I am s Ligure.

There isn't a breath of air, absolutely

I am drenched in sweat and for a few days I haven't stopped taking showers but without obtaining any lasting appreciable results. After much hesitation, I decided to follow the suggestion of my wife Fiorella and my grandson Jaiden and to start jotting down some notes on how my life has been up to today. I

\t will probably take me a long time before I write the final word, but I am not in a hurry.

Recently I read some passages by Marcel Proust: “In Search of Lost Time”, and this also convinced me.

Perhaps by rewriting my many years now passed, I can slow down time by decondensing the memory of short periods into real time. I will tell this life story without a specific structure; (I DO APOLOGIZE I AM NOT A PROFESSIONAL WRITER AND tY ENGLISH IS THE ITALIAN'S ONE!)

the narrative will follow what comes to mind from time to time and sometimes jump from one story to another. I apologize but to write it truly as I feel it. When you write something, you always ask yourself what and then why?

Certainly, this thing interests me because by doing so I relive cherished moments in my thoughts. I believe that thinking about one's past is like reliving a second time. The second answer is because I believe I have had an interesting life full of twists and turns, of which I would like to leave some trace to reread perhaps when my memory becomes fallible. But the final answer is that I am writing these lines essentially for my grandson so that even when many years have passed, he will have a trace of me and remember a world and a way of life that will no longer exist.

At the time, I am 65 years (year 2009) old and definitively retired last November. I have been happily married for 13 years (second marriage) to Fiorella, a dream woman I met on a chat when chatting and meeting a partner on the Internet was considered almost scandalous by most.

A meeting, back then, outside the norms that was considered almost something disreputable and therefore to be condemned a priori.

Girls are met in person and not on chats.

The meetings held on chats consisted only of direct chatting or exchanging emails.

Attachments like photos or other things that could allow one to visualize who they were chatting with were still impossible (to be invented).

So one was content with the description provided by the interlocutor.

Needless to talk about Skype or other audiovisual means that were marketed only years later. Personal computers back in 1995 (only 12 years ago, but when we talk about technological innovation it's almost an geological era, these were objects for a select few as costs were very high and therefore not accessible to many people).

PCs were mainly used in technologically advanced companies. Only a few years later (not many, to be honest) the PC began to become a mass tool and used for non-professional purposes.

For those who started like me, you will certainly remember the glorious Commodore 64 which was the true first mass PC.

In 1975 I was already using an advanced one for professional use, it was the first from Olivetti, the Programma 101.

The PC I mentioned above was my own (it cost me about 4 million of talian lire, the old Lire) including the software.

I remember that the modem had a maximum transmission speed of 10 Kb.! Very slow.

The main use of chats was certainly not to find a wife but simply to contact people and then perhaps meet in person, just as it has always happened, but with a means that was very new, the difference being that in this case, meetings were virtual.

Naturally, among the possible meetings were friends or even girls. Most of my life has been dedicated to work.

Unfortunately, I never had children of my own, and therefore having so much time available, I dedicated a lot of it to work. Work has always been a challenge with myself, first to do well and then also to be appreciated.

Giuliano came before my bosses and was a very strict person with himself..

I started working very young (I was only 13 years old) in the seasonal summer hotel environment in Alassio. More specifically, I started as a jack-of-all-trades, including dishwashing, at the then famous Ristorante La Palma in Alassio.

Back then, willing youngsters easily found work for the "summer tourist season" as helpers, bartenders, cooks, or waiters.

Some were students, doing these jobs only during the summer season, when chool were closed. others did it full-time, migrating during the winter to hotels or bars in the ski resorts of Bardonecchia, Curmaieur, Cervinia, or other important locations. In this way, they guaranteed themselves work for the entire year. T

hey were hired as "someone's helper" and then as they learned a trade, they advanced in their career until they had a specialization.

Back then we knew how to wait and give time to time so that things matured gradually. The season (in the years '58-'70 lasted from June to September and so did our seasonal work.

Schools resumed after the summer holidays around October 10th.

They were very long holidays.. for those who could afford them!

One must remember that those were the years immediately after the war. Italy had just emerged from the twenty years of fascism, had just been liberated by the partisans and the Anglo-Americans, and was one big construction site. Almost everything was being rebuilt.

It was the period when people left behind not only the years of the war but they left behind very bad times that seemed like centuries.

Until then, there had been no time to change
anything, before there wasn't a united and peaceful country.

The two world wars had demanded a lot from the young people of that time, and often their lives.

This time was also the beginning of that beautiful period called the economic boom or rather the economic miracle. T

he latter better captured the astonishment of people at so much well-being.

I was born in a small village in the hinterland of Albenga, Liguria (province of Savona) called Garlenda, which was only 12 kilometers from Albenga and 17 from Alassio, but back then that distance was like light-years from the way of thinking and living of the vacationers from Turin and Milan who began to crowd our beaches.

The economy of Garlenda was purely agricultural and also based on bartering.

If I'm not mistaken, the total number of inhabitants was around three hundred. Most had a small plot of land cultivated as a vegetable garden where they sowed the little they needed, but which was always very scarce!

I remember sometimes accompanying my mother by bicycle from Tadin, where she worked, to pick and then make bouquets of violets; from the harvest, they went directly to the local flower market and then took the route to the big cities.

Field work was a resource because one could then have a little cash. My mother was from Garlenda. She had finished elementary school and managed with reading and the arithmetic necessary to keep house accounts.

My family is of dignified but modest origins on both my father's and mother's side.

Although I must say that for those times my maternal grandparents had left my mother and uncle the house and some good pieces of cultivated land, this helped the economy but alone was not enough.

If you wanted to have liquid money, you had to go "by the day for others" working in the fields. In winter, women were busy collecting olives t by nude hands that fell to the ground and also harvesting flowers. Olive's collection nets to spread under the trees were not yet invented.

The winters were very cold and even colder because the only means of heating was a stove or fireplace that burned wood, which we, very young boys, little more than children, had to get daily by cutting shrubs in the hills above the village.

No gas cylinders, diesel fuel, radiators, or anything else, just wood.

The doors and windows of the houses let in cold drafts everywhere. My maternal grandmother, Nonna Ernestina, is the person who raised me while my mother was absent working in the fields by the day.

My grandmother was a tall, well-built person; at the time of my childhood memories, she was about 70-75 years old. She no longer worked, although exceptionally she would do a day's work for Pietrina the tobacconist. She was called that because she had the tobacco shop.

I have many beautiful memories of my grandmother. Grandmothers leave an indelible mark. Many things she taught me I still remember and use. The first thing of all was to stay out of trouble. She always said that the mother of trouble is always pregnant.

My grandmother died at 81 and left an incredible void. She was the first person who died in my arms. What a terrible experience for a 17-year-old boy! But these are experiences that are photographically fixed in memory, and you will remember all the details for the rest of your life.

For many nights I only dreamed of that moment, and it was always a nightmare. I firmly believe that on the day she died, she waited for me until I reached her bedside.

I was already working the season in Alassio; my father came to pick me up on his motorcycle, telling me how serious the situation was. When we arrived below the house, I ran up the stairs in a single bound to be quick. My grandmother was rattling and her face had already taken on the typical cadaverous pallor of someone going into an irreversible coma.

I squeezed her hand, whispered something crying, and she opened her eyes for a fraction of a second, and I had the strong feeling that she had recognized me, she gave me a slight smile, squeezed my hand, and immediately breathed her last.

It was June 5, 1961, at 4:10 PM, and I will never forget this date. Those voids cannot be filled with just any fullness. They are there and remain forever.

In those years, our sustenance was based heavily on vegetables grown in our own garden. Protein was guaranteed by the animals we kept in the stable. Nonna Ernestina always took care of the household animals, the chickens, the rabbits, and the little goat.

My favorite milk was goat's milk. It has a very special flavor, and I was crazy about it.

In the morning, breakfast was boiled milk with a drop of coffee made from chicory and stale bread toasted on the stove top. Everything was delicious. We had nothing else!

I remember when the first gas stove was installed. Margherita (Lella's mother, my great friend forever) sold it with the cylinders. With the arrival of the gas stove, life changed in an instant. Just open the gas tap and light the stove flame and the job was done!

Strange? Yes, strange but true, absolutely true that a tiny flame can change people's lives so radically. Lighting the stove was just an instant, while lighting the wood stove took, when you were lucky, half an hour, and you almost always ended up with tears in your eyes from the smoke that came out! And before you could light the stove, you had to stock up on wood by going to cut it in the woods, equipped with tools and lots of good will.

Cutting wood was the task of the boys who, after school, in the afternoon, would go to the woods in groups of 5 or 6, equipped with pickaxes and mattocks.

The former were used to cut shrubs and the latter to dig holes in the ground to uproot heather stumps, which were very prized because, once lit, they heated more than wood and lasted a long time.

Fortunately, the woods in Garlenda are not far; Garlenda, in fact, derives from *ghirlanda*, meaning surrounded by wooded hills. After the work of cutting or uprooting, each boy would descend with his load towards home, which was barely enough to meet the needs for fire to cook and perhaps heat for the entire evening.

After dinner, around 8 PM, in winter, we would go to bed. In winter, to survive the freezing cold sheets, we would put refractory bricks to heat in the stove's oven, and then these, wrapped in a piece of cloth, were placed under the sheets and we would warm our feet until the bricks had the last residual heat.

And so we would fall asleep. No TV, nothing at all of what we have today. We had a radio since the time (my father told me) of Radio London. I remember the chirping of the little bird that preceded the program changes of RAI or announced the radio news.

Often one wonders if the standard of living has improved over the last 50 years; well, I believe that by reading the above, a positive answer is found that leaves no doubt whatsoever. And it will be a full yes.

People over 50 today can all bear witness to this.

My father's name was Aldo, and he was an excellent person, and I loved him very much. For those times, he was privileged because he had a permanent position at the Piaggio aeronautical company in Finale Ligure, his birthplace.

He had only finished elementary school, but his technical intelligence, good apprenticeship, and desire to learn and do had promoted him to head of the wings and fuselages department.

He had a fixed salary, but it was not enough to get by. This was to the point that groceries purchased from

Giacumin and Anita's and Angiulin and Renata's shops were, by almost everyone, bought "on credit," meaning they would pay later and it was written in a "little book" which was a kind of credit card of the time, paying a little each month and then settling the remainder as soon as possible, which in our case was in December when Papa's thirteenth-month salary arrived.

That's why there was the thirteenth month, and why it was invented! It was a forced saving that, given once a year, in December before Christmas, ensured a decent Christmas and also settled debts. To go to work from Garlenda to Finale, Papa covered the thirty kilometers distance with his 1951 Vespa and then with the Mival 125, and later (when things had already improved) with his Fiat 500 Giardiniera. The small historic car.

How cold those winters were! He, like everyone else back then, lived them on his own skin and never complained once. That's how it was, and you had to keep going. Complaining didn't help at all, not even to warm up a bit, and finally, upon arriving in Finale, a good hot espresso coffee at the station bar.

The same was true for returning home after work. That's what the 500 represented, the difference between cold and not cold especially!

Before, it was a privilege of very few! It was therefore a turning point accessible to many for a less meager life.

Papa was a very good and altruistic man with a very marked intelligence for mechanics. He was much appreciated at work and, compatible with his level of education, had a miraculous career. Papa had only one true passion: fishing.

It didn't matter where or when, but if he could have a rigged rod in his hand, he felt like he was in paradise. He fished both in the stream below the house and in the sea from the beach or by boat with friends. He was considered a Guru. He fished for chubs, tench (back then the Lerrone stream was very rich in fish), and in the sea, he caught sea bass, and sargo.

I preferred the latter.

My parents, but my mother especially, always encouraged me to study and do everything possible to improve my lot.

She understood well that studying would make a difference. Yes, Mama Erminia was right, and Papa supported her in all this. I always wanted to study at least as long as I could. Yes, as much as I could, because even back then, attending high school required a lot of money, enrollment, books, notebooks, school fees, bus pass, food, etc., and it wasn't always possible for a family to face such expenses.

For someone from a less well-off family like mine, it was imperative to work hard during the summer season to earn some cash to survive and help the family during the winter and the school year.

Now I no longer see our young people working the seasons like we did. I don't know if this is good or bad for them, but instead, you see many non-EU citizens doing it. Perhaps we were "non-EU citizens" in our own home back then?

I have an older brother, 5 years older than me, named Piero, but we call him Pierin, whom I adore and have always missed very much because he lived with our paternal grandparents in Finale Ligure Borgo.

Papa married twice. From his first wife, Piero, my brother, was born. Life initially physically separated us, but as we grew older, we were united by a very strong bond that still lasts today.

Piero, my brother, has always been my example to copy. Like my father, he knows how to do everything, absolutely everything. He is good at mechanics and every other trade that can be useful for keeping a house running smoothly.

As boys, even though we didn't live under the same roof, we did similar things and jobs. Piero, like Papa, was employed at Piaggio in the technical office. And like Papa, he was always highly appreciated at work.

He married Luciana, a woman he adore, whom he has indeed always adored.

They had two sons, Mauro and Alessandro. They are the only nephews I have had. They are good boys with a big heart and very high moral integrity, the result of the good education received in the family. They have ensured continuity to the family by marrying Monica and Simona respectively, who have given me two beautiful great-grandnephew Francesco and Asia. Thanks to them, I can say that I have been lucky to have a beautiful original family.

The municipality of Garlenda had only elementary schools, while vocational training schools and middle schools were in Albenga or in neighboring riverside municipalities with larger populations.

So I did elementary school in Garlenda. I remember my first day of school as if it were yesterday. There were only 5 of us, three girls and only two boys. I want to remember them by name, Franca, Annamaria, Cecilia, Domenico, and myself. The elementary school was taught by a teacher, Mrs. Elisa Cappelli, who taught from first to third grade, and her husband, the teacher Alfredo Maurizio, known as "u bestasin," who taught fourth and fifth grade. They were legendary teachers.

I remember them with great affection and gratitude for how good the foundations they both were able to give us were, and how many values they were able to cultivate in us. I'll give you just one example to understand: In fifth grade, they taught us how to set up and solve first-degree equations! Usually, this was done in the third year of middle school! From elementary school, I remember the choral singing lessons. Maestro Maurizio was a former Alpino from the 1915/18 war and had a real passion for Alpine military mountain songs. Every day or almost every day, he would have us sing a chorus. They were beautiful moments, and we boys had a lot of fun! And I still remember those songs by heart!

It was a real team-building moment.

These excellent people stay in your memory for life! They took the mission of teaching very seriously. The married teachers had no children, and that is why they mentally adopted all of us with so much love.

Note that in those days, anyone who didn't toe the line and didn't do their duty well was solemnly failed without any mercy. This is how they prepared children for the harshness of life! Middle schools or high schools, however, post-elementary schools, were in the valley floor.

For us boys, going to Albenga or Alassio was difficult because the means of transport was a bus.

The bus was at 8 AM towards Albenga, at 1:30 PM. The return was at 1 PM and 6:30 PM. The times were coordinated to coincide with the beginning and end of the school day in Albenga.

We kids back then, given the non-existent economy, looked for every opportunity to work to help make ends meet, and clearly Alassio was a very strong attraction for us that offered opportunities to start working even with zero experience.

I don't want to be too serious, it was also a place that offered occasions for good fun.

So, being on the spot changed everything. Back then, apprenticeship existed, and it had an important social component where through it, investment was made in the continuity of future generations.

Young people were hired and patiently accompanied in the trade, and then, once capable, were able to guarantee the continuity of the trades.

Today, on the other hand, people are only hired with more than three years of experience, but who gives them this experience if no one invests in apprenticeship?

We boys, however, were very attentive to what was happening around us. The advent of television and the few things we could watch on the two televisions available in Garlenda in 1957 (the one at the after-work club, which was also the seat of the sports society) and the one of Don Arduino Luigi, our beloved parish priest.

TV stimulated our imagination which was then fuel for our projects, both for play and for life. The question was always the same: is all this possible for us too?

I remember with so much love the figure of our Parish Priest who had devised an infallible method to give us access to the rectory's TV. To the boys who went to Mass and Sunday catechism, he would distribute stamped and signed cards (passes) which he would then collect in the afternoon at the entrance door to the TV room. No Mass, no pass.

...no TV, and so we missed Rin Tin Tin and the adventures of young

Corporal Rusty. Rin Tin Tin was a TV series with the German Shepherd dog from which the series name came.

It was set in the Wild West at an American fort; we kids were crazy about this series, consequently, on Sunday, everyone went to Mass. In our games, we simulated the deeds of these two little heroes! That was the time, we start dreaming America!

Now I can say that our parish priest knew how to do it, and how well he knew how to do it! Don Arduino was super technological, he had all the gadgets of the time... to attract young people. Suffice it to say that the first television broadcasts were in 1954!

The other things we saw on Black and White TV were already part of the transforming Italy that we imagined could become ours on condition that... It is precisely that conditional that stimulated our fantasy and sharpened our ingenuity.

Necessity sharpens ingenuity! In Naples, the *scugnizzi*, who are the most enterprising boys in Italy, know this well.

Much later in time, I verified that that "what if..." was also the basis of economic growth and the American miracle!

I was still in elementary school when, by bicycle, I started going to Alassio, just to see what was happening there.

Every time I visited Alassio, I was amazed; it was so beautiful and different from my village. I have a beautiful memory of the scents of the flowered dehor with tables along the side of the street of Alassio's bars. Especially at sunset when all the tables were full of customers enjoying an aperitif. Passing nearby, you could hear the background music diffused from loudspeakers hidden among the trees. Aperitif hour was the most important one, it was a ritual, of the vacationers' day, who after being at the beach would meet in front of their aperitif glass, confiding in each other how their day had just passed, but even more importantly because decisions were made planning what to do for the evening.

The bar tables were always crowded, everyone had Campari soda or Aperol, Martini or Cinzano as an aperitif.

These were the most popular drinks. Campari for the strong males and

Aperol served with sugar on the edge of the glass and a slice of orange, with a sweet and more delicate taste for the ladies; while all others were on Campari, Martini or Cinzano.

I remember a music that still plays in my ears: The Bridge on the River Kwai March. It was beautiful and I whistled it constantly when I was happy.

It was the soundtrack of the very famous film of the same name. It was the hit of that summer.

The customers had smiling and always very happy faces. They were on vacation and had probably made an effort to leave their troubles at home.

The people were very different from my fellow villagers; they had quite other thoughts on their minds, while the vacationers always had a good time!

The vacation, back then, was very long compared to today. It lasted a minimum of one month, but there were some who stayed for three months! Those who had the financial possibility had their vacation period synchronized with the entire summer school closing period.

The ladies took the opportunity to dress fashionably and, as dusk fell, parade their daughters in a beautiful display.

We would joke, looking at them, and say that they weren't taking their daughters for a walk, but rather their sumptuous clothes.

The promenade was a high fashion show. Casual didn't exist, and if someone was below the threshold considered elegant, they were immediately ostracized by harsh whispered comments.

The atmosphere was romantic; everything was refined, from the dehor to the cafe tables, with meticulous attention to detail, and you could feel a certain effervescence in the air. It seemed everyone was ready to spring towards something undefined. It was the desire to live and make up for a slumber that had lasted too long in the years before and after the Second World War.

It seemed the war had been over for a long time, but in reality, it was only about fifteen years.

The young people who were around 30 years old had spent a good 15-16 years under the regime and thought their time had come to make up for all that very dark period by finally starting to live and forget.

The economy was booming, the Lira had started circulating, and so what? What should they do, those who could afford it, if not fully enjoy the beautiful summer seasons?

I liked one place more than any other, for how it was finished, for the well-chosen colors, for the joy it gave, and the music it spread. I considered it a piece of art precisely for these sensations it gave me.

This place was superior to every other in every aspect. Every time I passed by, I wondered if I would ever be able to work in that beautiful Café Roma, where the Muretto and Miss Muretto were invented, and serve those clients who had managed to make, with their experience, so much fortune.

They say dreams are useful, and I dreamed of working at the Roma. I had put that dream away in my drawer.

The decorations of that place were meticulous and referred to scenes from the Roman Empire with copies of capitals and columns drawn here and there by a very skilled hand.

Everything inside was a work of art. Including the parrot Pedrito who perched on his stand in a niche at the entrance to the billiards game room specially prepared for him.

He was a gift from Ernest Hemingway to Café Roma and Mario

Berrino. The seasons in Liguria, in those years, lasted much longer than today, consequently increasing the seasonal earnings that the boys made.

I remember my first job. I was 13 years old (at that time, working as a young boy was not considered (fortunately for us) exploitation, but rather, it was perceived as having opportunities.

I had found this job as a handyman in a very well-known restaurant in Alassio, through a friend, older than me, who already worked as a kitchen helper. The work lasted from 12 to 14 hours a day and the pay, including room and board, was 1000 Lire per month. (just like the famous song... but this one was written 30 years earlier!)

It wasn't much money but always much more than nothing at all. Without considering that I could learn a job to keep in reserve if my academic ambitions failed.

Back then, an apprentice meant this; above all, it was not understood that people had to been born already learned. In some way, they were given the opportunity to grow. So it was for me too.

The following year, strong with what I had learned, I was hired by the legendary place called Il Gallo Nero. Il Gallo Nero was a Hotel, restaurant, cafeteria with a hot table bar that operated 24 hours a day.

The place overlooked the public gardens where there was also an outdoor cinema at that time. Signor Petitti's Gallo Nero was able to satisfy the needs of those who went to the first mass until the last of the night owls.

The place was always full. In particular, of boys my age, especially from Turin, who spent the evenings (all together, just like now) talking and drinking some Scotch whisky.

Their preferred meeting spot was in the somewhat secluded dehor, around a couple of rocking chairs covered in red canvas and with an umbrella nearby to open in case of rain.

The young people were quite nocturnal, just like our young people today, and so that umbrella was never used by them to shelter from the sun! I remember the Brambilla family from Milan (who let me drive the first Fiat 600 car even though I didn't have a license), the Avogadro family

(Paola, with whom I was secretly a little in love) from Turin, and the faces of many, many other dear young people.

I say dear because they were also my friends and they never made me feel the social difference between them and me. Those were children of gentlemen, and not just of wealth! The working hours were very hard. Seven days a week. No weekly rest and an average of 12 hours a day. At the Gallo Nero, I had been hired as a bartender's helper. I worked with a gentleman from Turin (of whom I only remember the name Signor Enrico) and his son Sergio, who was very young, perhaps a couple of years older than me. Signor Enrico was a very expert barman, who worked in Turin at the Bar degli avvocati, (lawyer’s bar) and I had immediately understood this from how he prepared things and how he organized his work and moved behind the counter.

The father and son pair was very close. They never made a non-synchronized movement and above all, they were always very attentive to the customers. They managed to understand what they wanted just by observing their gaze. True phenomena!

I realized I would have to stick close to them to "steal" the trade. The school was certainly excellent! As my experience grew, I was entrusted with increasingly greater tasks, up to the complete management of the bar, which I reached the following season.

Don't think that organizing the life of a large bar is such a simple thing.

Beyond knowing how to make coffee and cocktails, you have to plan all supplies, manage 24-hour logistics, place merchandise orders for a week... and so on. In short, a small business within the business.

I don't want to exaggerate, but I think it will have happened to you to be served at a bar and immediately understand how the wind blows. If a bar works well, you understand it immediately upon first impact.

If they put the lemon peel on or if they present the coffee cup with the handle in position, it makes a difference, and so for a multitude of details that make the trade an art.

Signor Enrico practiced art! Many people from the Piedmontese or Lombard plains had sold their farms and moved to the Riviera, investing in bars, restaurants, and guesthouses without having the slightest idea about working in tourism.

Some of these new businesses survived, but very many failed miserably. As with all trades, running a bar or restaurant is not improvised but requires good preparation.

Customers know exactly what they want, but unfortunately, the managers sometimes do not!

After two years, I had learned the bartender's trade well and was "graduated" by Signor Enrico. My dream of finally being able to present myself at the Café (I love writing it with one 'f') Roma with something valid to offer to be hired was now more concrete.

I remember presenting myself just before Easter 1961 to Signor Mario Berrino (one of the legendary owners of the Roma) asking if they needed a bartender for the new season. He, I remember that meeting as if only a few days had passed, looked at me and asked what experience I had. I told him my resume, said I was a student and would only work seasonally. He listened to me and said you are very young and... you could be or become a good runner.

This answer stemmed from the fact that in his youth he had dabbled as a cyclist. When he wanted to say that someone could do well and also play as a team, he would say precisely that "you are a good runner". In short, Signor Mario, to my infinite happiness, hired me on probation, and

I did my utmost to make a good impression and guarantee my spot.

Signor Mario was the third of the four Berrino brothers. As many know, he is a great painter and many, many other things that I will try to tell you about.

Elio was the first of the brothers. He was the morning man. He took care of the company accounting and "Opening the Place"; I've put it in quotes because the Roma never closed. It was always full of people at any hour, day and night, and operated 7x24. In modern industry, everything runs 7 days for 24 hours, but they achieved this goal a quarter of a century after the Café Roma! Elio was the man of accounting and finance. Apart from the early hours of the morning, he spent his life in the office.

After I had been working at the Roma for some time, I discovered that Elio was my father's comrade in the air force in Fontanarossa di Catania in Sicily.

They were both born in 1918 and had a great passion in common: fishing. They then cultivated this passion together as very good friends for many years, fishing for tuna with the legendary boat Cin-Cin.

Giorgio was the second of the brothers. He took care of artists and personnel. When I talk about artists, I mean those with a capital "A". To understand, you need to know that the Café Roma was a complex of three activities: Café room, Roof Garden, and Night club dancing, plus a recreational games room called the billiards room.

The Café was able to serve aperitifs to more than 1000 people per evening. The Roof Garden featured the best shows of the time.

All the great singers and various artists of the time performed at the Roof Garden. Many of the greats of the time passed through there, had their evening of honor, and all signed their tile on the Muretto of Alassio. I will talk about the Muretto later. Reading the tiles on the Muretto of Alassio is probably the only thing that truly gives an idea of the importance of this place.

All the greatest performance and visual artists have passed through the Roof Garden of the Roma to sign the tile. The Night Club where a variety show was held at midnight but without any trace of hostess girls or stripteases. At that time, certain things were only seen in certain venues in big cities. The choice made at the Roma was completely respectful of the morality of the time.

It was a luxurious dance hall in the basement for respectable people and nothing else. The Roof Garden of the Roma offered a splendid variety show with top national and international artists and worked in conjunction with the Roof Garden of the Casino of San Remo.

I don't know if it was by contract or Giorgio's foresight, but the fact is that almost all artists performed equally in turns at the two very famous venues. Consider that at the time the Roof Garden opened, the waiting line for entry, every evening, exceeded three hundred meters. It started from the Caffe' 900, passed in front of the train station, and snaked up to the Roof Garden elevators!

Finally, the fourth brother is Adriano. He specialized in and managed the very well-stocked cellar.

Adriano was the youngest, but in terms of experience with wines and beverages, he was already a professor. Among other things, he was the inventor of the famous Muretto cocktail. From him, I learned a fundamental thing: even the smallest waste is money thrown in the bin! If only our various administrations would adopt this concept! As you can understand, the four brothers together had extraordinary business entrepreneurial knowledge. They were very modern managers who today would be highly sought after on the market.

The city of Alassio owes a lot to the activity and intelligence of these brothers. And for those, like me, who saw things from the inside for 7 years, can testify that the great Alassio was made so by the Berrinos. Those of my age who remember those good times will certainly agree with me.

Not a day went by without an article in the national press talking about Alassio and the initiatives of the Roma.

The Berrinos knew well that systematically getting Alassio talked about in the press contributed to establishing the city and the tourism industry, which was the only thing the city had to sell!

They succeeded wonderfully, and today it is still the most famous city on the Riviera, and one I prefer to the others, all of which are also beautiful.

I spent seven seasons of my youth at the Roma, and it was the best period of my life. The Berrino brothers had the patience to wait for me at the end of each school year, respecting me and letting me work with dignity each season.

They knew I was studying and that I needed to work to support my studies. And they viewed this with a very kind eye.

The Berrinos always treated me with affection and kindness. I, for my part, tried to reciprocate by working honestly and diligently, and I did everything possible to help them find valid staff at various levels, right there in Garlenda.

They said I was a good example to follow. In fact, many of my fellow villagers, after me, found work in this company. In the meantime, as I grew, I learned, observed, and treasured what I learned. At the Cafe Roma, I had the opportunity to meet many illustrious guests who were guests of this great venue.

Among the most beautiful memories are the many evenings spent at the Roof Garden with distinguished guests such as Salvatore Quasimodo, Milena Milani, Gilberto Govi, Mike Bongiorno, Lucio Flauto. Fred Bongusto, Gino Bechi, Tony Renis the author and singer of thr song " Dimmi quando to verrai" . The painter Lucio Fontana, and many others whose autographed tiles can be read on the Muretto.

There are many, all talented and famous. Many of them are now deceased. Every celebrity guest had their gala evening. Every time I pass in front of the Muretto, I reread the autograph tiles so well aligned and preserved, the names bring to mind the beautiful evenings spent after the show at the Roof Garden, in their honor, for the autograph on the tile to be cemented onto the Muretto.

These famous people were always available to meet and answer questions from the Café customers and also from us serving staff.

That's how I shook hands with many well-known figures. I always feel a certain melancholy when I pass in front of the Muretto, rereading all those signatures. It seems like watching an old cinema weekly from the Istituto Luce, of which I was also a part, even if only marginally.

The Muretto of Alassio, in front of Café Roma, as I already mentioned was another great intuition of Mario Berrino and the writer Ernest Hemingway.

Initially, the wall was just a simple wall across the street opposite the Café where young people would meet and perch to chat.

That's why the current statue on the Muretto represents two young people sitting and embracing. Later, after Mario's initiative, it became famous with all its signed tiles glued onto it by many greats in every field. Thinking about it, the Muretto is similar to Sunset Boulevard in Los Angeles, with the difference that for me, having seen , later on, both, the Muretto turned out better.

It's also more beautiful because it was born spontaneously from observing those young people who, at dusk, would sit embraced with their legs dangling, chatting and spending time together.

I hope this monument remains for a long time, and with it, all the history of that time that began after the war when a breath of fresh air was equivalent to a month's vacation in the Dolomites. I

am sure that anyone of my age who reads this story about the Muretto will be moved because it represents a piece of very beautiful history that we had the honor and privilege of helping to create.

When things had already changed significantly for the better, the means of transport for the luckiest was called "The four weels little Box," that's what they called the Fiat 500, which well represents everything about those times. As I already wrote in the paragraph about my father, this small car ignited the hopes of many people. It constituted an achievable goal and therefore one to pursue. With the facilitation of payment in installments with a promissory note, this vehicle had become accessible to anyone who had a fixed, and not necessarily high, salary.

With the increase in welfare, our personal and the Italian economy also grew. We owned much less than we do now, but we were certainly happier.

This was not only because we were younger!

Hope and willpower were our drugs.

We did things because we believed in them. Period.

I am happy that "the little box" has been celebrated since '84 by a prestigious 500 Club Italia in the village where I was born, Garlenda, and that this great symbol full of meanings of our youth is kept alive.

Every year in early July, about a thousand Fiat 500 cars from all over the world gather in Garlenda and celebrate throughout the weekend, comparing their beautiful vintage cars and the older ones telling their stories related to this car.

I believe that the affection for this old car is due to the fact that it represents our origins; it is a love for the past that all of us desired to possess. This feeling is and continues to be within us.

The 500 Italia Club was conceived by a great person and friend of the same age, Domenico Romano, who imagined this enormously successful club simply by following his inner passion and combining it with his managerial skills and his stubbornness.

This club actually wants to celebrate a transition from post-war Italy to the Italy of reconstruction and well-being that I described shortly before.

The Fiat 500 was the tangible means. By founding this Club, Domenico wanted this historical moment to remain in the memory of the younger generations.

I must say he succeeded wonderfully.

Alassio's nightlife.

At the heart of the nightlife for young people in Alassio and Laigueglia were two outdoor dance halls: La Capannina and Villa Romana.

The youngsters would frequent them in turns. But some of them were pro-Capannina and others pro-Villa Romana with no possibility of changing their minds.

Back then, girls, after dinner, wore truly elegant evening dresses. This was true for all girls, but especially for the Roma's customers.

Our girls were certainly the most beautiful, and we were very proud of our customers. After dinner, the youngsters would go out in droves and gather in small groups in front of the Muretto to confabulate and plan what to do for the evening.

Then around 10 PM, everyone headed to the dance clubs. Late at night after dancing, they would start arriving at the Roma, hungry as lions, and begin replenishing themselves with all kinds of hot table food.

It was thus that Adriano came up with the idea of inventing the pasta called "al Brucciolo," which then became the "summer" dish par excellence. Everyone started ordering it. It was good, satisfying, and not expensive. It consisted of a plate of spaghetti with a light pesto quickly sautéed in a pan (hence "il brucciolo").

The luckiest would arrive late at night with a girl on their arm, who was perhaps their new summer conquest. You could tell it was so by how they moved with a proud air and looked around to see if their conquest had been noticed.

How many loves born and how many ended before our eyes!

I remember a great and friendly character who has now left us, the great painter Giovanni Fiore, known as GiFio, who had invented a secret code to ask the young people if their evening with the girl had gone well according to expectations.

Indeed, he always sat at a table near the entrance with other friends from Alassio, and would rub his nose with his left hand, the other person, upon entering, if everything had gone well, would respond by making the same gesture but with the opposite hand, and there would be endless laughter!

Every nights at the closing of the Villa Romana and Capannina dance clubs, the Cafe Roma was the last stop or if you like, the first stop of the new day; it was the funnel that brought together all the night owls for the final snack or the final drink.

I remember one year the Capannina team, led by the famous and dear to me Lucio Flauto, who left us some time ago, and the Villa Romana team, led by Don Marino Bareto. These two groups were in perennial conflict throughout the season. I never understood why, but as soon as they crossed paths, terrible punches flew and lasted for a few minutes. We staff, for safety reasons, would quickly close the very heavy metal shutters, and to possibly defend the cash, we would hold in our hands (without being too obvious) the cast iron key of the Carpigiani ice cream machine, which alone weighed three or four kilos.

Fortunately, we never had to use it for defense.

But as they say... "just in case"..

As I said, after a few minutes of punches, the waters would calm, the shutters were reopened, and inexplicably the two rival groups would calm down and start eating the good Brucciolo together in peace. However, the peace would only last until dawn, but the next night, everything would start over..

One evening, the group did something that my friend Alfio really didn't like.

Alfio was a Tuscan boy who spent the whole season in Alassio.

I think he was 23 years old. He performed in some shows at the Roof Garden with his beautiful Swedish girlfriend, dancing the Twist, of which he was the Italian champion. Anyway, a polite boy with a heart of gold. That evening, the two rival groups targeted a lady who had the misfortune of being there by chance and sitting at a table, already cleared.

The group started playing some tricks on the lady, who initially enjoyed herself. Then the joke went too far, to the point of her insistently asking to be left alone.

Unfortunately, things had gotten out of hand, and the joke continued against her will. Nothing truly drastic, but the little group pretended to be a production team from Cinecittà and that they wanted to cast her, but for this, they needed to do an audition right there.

I am not allowed to know what the requested audition was about. Alfio, who was sitting at a nearby table with his girlfriend, was disgusted and asked the group of about fifteen people to stop, as what they were doing was uncivilized.

They were joking, but in a rather heavy way. Of course, a few too many drinks were the cause, as in normal life none of them would have dared to play tricks on a lady.

Anyway, it happened that a certain Franco, a gentleman who, given his size, could have done wrestling, along with at least six or seven others, moved against Alfio to beat him up. They hit Alfio with the first slap, but then things didn't stop there. Alfio began to hit so hard and at such a speed that not even Bud Spencer could have done more or better. The result was that he beat them like drums, all seven of them, four of whom had to go to the local hospital's emergency room. Afterwards, they told people they had been in a car accident!

Similar jokes to ladies were never made again! Back then, at least one boy showed he had guts and was capable of defending a woman in difficulty. His gesture, heroic to me, should be emulated especially nowadays! I remained a great admirer and friend of Alfio for many years to come, then as with almost all friends of that time, our paths diverged, and we lost touch. The lady continued to frequent the place and later even became a true friend of that little group of people, and she spent many more evenings with them. Back then you understood if you went too far, and you stopped in time immediately!

If only we had stopped there. Unfortunately, today's newspapers tell us that we have gone beyond, too far beyond!

The Artists.

A very nice and talented person I remember fondly is the very famous and talented magician Silvan. He started working at the Roma when he also did the opening titles for the television show linked to Canzonissima called Scala Reale. He had performed in Las Vegas, was good, and proved it throughout his brilliant television career.

I believe he worked at the Roof Garden for three seasons. I was a waiter at the Roof Garden at that time. I've always loved "sleight of hand" shows, and during the performance, I did everything I could to figure out his tricks. Even after many evenings of observation from every possible angle, some tricks remained secret, and despite my insistence, Silvan never revealed them to me. He is a great artist.

I remember the tenor Enzo Gallo, who sang every evening and drove all the spectators wild with joy with the most famous Italian opera arias. Thanks to him and my father, I became an opera fan.

O' sole mio was his signature piece and encore, and our foreign guests went crazy for him. Thinking of this artist, I remember the biggest blunder I ever made as a waiter. The tenor Gallo was singing O' sole mio and was right at the final high note while I was struggling with a bottle of Champagne whose cork just wouldn't come out. Suddenly, the cork shot out with a deafening bang, and not only that, the cork traveled a long trajectory and ended up hitting the corrugated metal sheet of the stage roof, which was directly above the great tenor's head, with a loud *taaac*. And with that, he stopped right on the high note.

Disaster! Gallo looked at me with a face I cannot describe. I, red-faced and furious, wanted to sink with shame, then I improvised a deep bow towards the tenor and the audience and began clapping my hands very hard and smiling, I said thank you! The entire audience began to clap, and everything ended without consequences.

The presenter, Nello Airaldi, at the end of the performance, said that the most difficult part of the show was training the waiter (me) to open the bottle at the right moment and hit exactly that metal sheet! Everyone laughed kindly, and for one evening, my face burning, I became a mini protagonist. Once again, I managed to get out of a tight spot.

Gallo didn't speak to me for at least a month but then he forgave me!

I remember the great Alassio presenter, very professional and much loved, Nello Airaldi, who opened the evening with "Good evening to all the ladies" in all languages and closed the evening singing "Byby goodby Alassio." A special memory for the great pianist Enzo Freda who enlivened the afternoons and evenings of the cafe's tea room on the ground floor.

Enzo Freda had refined clients, just as the music of his piano was. Every afternoon and evening, they would sit in a circle and enjoy hours of wonderful piano music. In my opinion, he was even better than the famous Clayderman.

I would like to reveal a small and pleasant secret about this artist, who has also passed away. You should know that the universal custom for customers to thank the pianist was to offer him a drink of his choice. Maestro Freda always accepted a French cognac, which he said was Martell. In reality, so as not to get him drunk, we would serve him only a small glass of colored water with a drop of Martini Rosso vermouth, which in the end gave it the color of cognac, and which the waiter would bring him. The Maestro, on some evenings, could be offered up to 10 cognacs per evening.

Imagine the effect on him if this trick hadn't been used. At the time, I was seeing a beautiful and kind girl with green eyes, who chose our song, which was "Tu sei quello" sung by Orietta Berti. The song had gotten into me, and I often hummed it because I loved that girl very much.

Maestro Freda knew my story and from time to time dedicated that song to me on the piano. Like every piece he played, he played it divinely. When I asked him to play it, he would usually oblige, but that evening, there was nothing to be done.

He had absolutely refused to play it for me. It occurred to me then to send him a message. For the moment, just one. I gave him a real cognac instead of the usual colored water with Martini. The Maestro was naturally almost a teetotaler. To worsen the situation that was being created, the group of customers offering the drink were sitting right around the piano, forming a circle and blocking any possible escape route for the Maestro, and thus upon the arrival of the drink, the group would toast with a "cincin" with the Maestro, making it impossible for him not to drink or simulate drinking.

I didn't miss the grimace on the Maestro's face when he took the first drop of Cognac. However, almost with tears in his eyes, he swallowed the entire contents of the glass and began playing again. I, with a nod, asked him again to play my song, but he, undeterred and a little red in the face, continued to refuse. The ritual of offering a drink to the Maestro, that evening, was repeated 7 times, and 7 times I served real

'cognac. It resembled a story from a Wild West saloon. I did not get my song.

The Maestro was escorted home staggering. He passed by the counter and didn't greet me! Both of us were convinced that we hadn't let the other win. The Berrinos probably wouldn't have been very happy if they had known about it. 40 years have passed, and my crime is now statute-barred! The matter ended there because from that day on, I learned to moderate my requests, thus finding an amicable agreement with the Maestro that we mutually respected in the future.

Writing these little memories moves me because they are a part of me. And they bring to mind many dear people, many of whom have already passed away.

Forgive me, but these are facts from my youth, and I always feel so much emotion remembering them. Working at the Roma was a 360-degree experience! When I think of something beautiful from my youth, I cannot help but think of the experience I had at the Cafe Roma in Alassio. The enthusiasm was such that it made us all indefatigable. We earned very well compared to colleagues who worked at competing venues.

Alassio, year after year, also due to the great resonance given by Cafe Roma and the Muretto which filled the media every season, became a great city.

Many characteristic venues of that time have now disappeared to make way for things that better suit the tastes of young people today. One thing is certain: the Muretto will remain to testify to the sixties and seventies for a long time to come. The Cafe Roma didn't always have a smooth road with the Municipality when proposing initiatives. I

remember, in fact, that for a time it was forbidden (right in front of the entrance door) to place tables on the sidewalk (where they had always been), claiming that they obstructed car parking.

The Roma removed the tables and chairs, but in response (in a witty way) parked a wagon (one of those long, 4-wheeled ones pulled by oxen) where customers could sit on the side, sipping their aperitif! It was a wagon and not a table! True, absolutely true! Everything was then clarified, and things returned to normal. The Cafè Roma, as I write, still exists there, but I cannot reconcile it with the legendary cafe that made at least three generations of young Ligurians, Milanese, and Turinese dream and have fun, who then, working hard, were able to build and make Italy great.

Who would have ever said that back then? (Note: Mario Berrino passed away at the age of 90 in August 2011, and I apologize if I talk about him as if he were still alive. At the time of the first draft of this story, started in 2009, he was still alive). The Great Maestro Mario Berrino created his gallery of beautiful paintings in a southern part of the old cafe. Mario's smile when he remembers those times reveals the fulfilled dream of his life. The Berrino team was made up of excellent "runners"!

I remember finishing work at three in the morning at the Roof Garden, and Mario was then painting the pictures that were going to decorate the new ship Angelina Lauro (I think), which was being fitted out in the Genoa dockyard. After working, I still had the strength (blessed youth!) to load some pictures onto the Fiat 500 Giardiniera to deliver them to Genoa to be displayed on the new ship. I felt as important as if I had painted those pictures myself! Sometimes Mario would let me watch him paint. His art was expressed optimally with a spatula. He was formidable; he was capable of making very colorful and beautiful paintings in a very short time using only the spatula. I preferred his marine subjects and cascades of flowers.

Once again, heartfelt thanks for everything to Mario and all the Berrino family to whom I owe a great deal. The years passed quickly; each season began in June and ended for me the day before school started. I remember having to sign promissory notes for the fees and books, which I would then pay during the summer with the proceeds from the season. Back then, nothing was free; everything was hard-earned.

I then graduated from the private institute C. Ferrini in Albenga

diploma in Industrial Chemistry in 1964. That year, a terrible recession had begun. Companies had stopped the growth of previous years, and even for chemical experts, who until then were highly sought after, there were no job openings. That year, my parents decided to move from Garlenda to Alassio, and everything was much more convenient and simple.

Returning home every night after many hours of work on my Vespa was sometimes dangerous, and yet I was very happy with this commute.

It's as if my family had left behind years of hard history and life from the old house.

Now I appreciate how much good God has given me, also because I know well that I haven't always had the comforts of today, and I have never forgotten my conditions and origins.

Part Two

So, in the Albenga area, the secondary schools were Le Magistrali (teacher training), the Licei (high schools), the accountants, and Don Lasagna's chemical experts. The ITI C. Ferrini was called that because the institute was founded by the Reverend Prof. Don Lasagna.

He was a man who, in addition to the typical mission of priests, wanted to found a school for chemical and electronic experts in the Albenga area to provide an opportunity for the young people of Albenga and the valley who wanted a technical career in factories.

Students enrolled from our valley but also from other parts of the Riviera and from all over Italy.

Ferrini was a legendary school, for better or for worse, and so too was Don Lasagna.

He was deeply loved by some, myself included, and also hated by a few others.

In reality, inventing a school of chemistry and one of electronics, managing to finance the investments for buildings and laboratories that were state-of-the-art at the time, was not simple. Don Lasagna succeeded.

From there came out people who later became famous, like Renato Curcio. I clearly knew him, and he was a model student at the time. Then he went to Sociology at the University of Trento, and the news and history, and he himself, have told us the rest of his life.

Ferrini, being a state-recognized school, had to take its students for the final exams at the state institute in Savona.

Every year it was a tremendous struggle to glean information about their teachers and what they were preparing for the state exam. The teachers were excellent and prepared us well for industry and life.

I always hold dear Professor Ciocca for Chemistry, Engineer Valle for Electronics, and Professor Testa for Natural Sciences, who later became the mayor of Alassio.

In particular, those who knew him remember Don Lasagna, who besides being the principal, was also

a professor of Physics and Chemical Physics, a genius for how much he knew and how well he could teach it.

He always maintained that someone who knows a subject well, however difficult it might be, can explain and teach it with simple examples and terms accessible to everyone. In short, a Galilean. Someone who doesn't know things well, on the other hand, confuses students by using abstruse terms whose true meaning they almost never know.

On the other hand, Galileo said that Physics is studied by observing phenomena in the street.

Never were truer words spoken.

In my working life, I would deeply deal with scientific subjects, and I had the opportunity to verify how true the statements of poor Don Lasagna were.

He died, if I remember correctly, around the turn of the 1970s, and ironically, for a chemical physicist, from inhaling carbon dioxide leakage from a water heater.

Everyone missed him. I was already in Milan at the time and heard about it later.

Later on, I went to the cemetery in Castelletto d'Orba to bring a flower of thanks to his grave. Many young people without his initiative to create that school would never have achieved their potential. Myself included.

Attending the school was demanding. This was especially true if one couldn't take a break between seasonal work and the start of school.

We attended 6 days a week, including Saturday, until 5 in the evening.

Saturday afternoon was dedicated to the chemical analysis laboratory.

Often on the weekend, I worked as a waiter at some dance hall to supplement my income.

The school, as I said, was private, and the tuition was expensive, so much so that I had to sign promissory notes and then honor them during the summer months with the earnings from seasonal work.

During the winter, I worked on weekends at the Villanova function hall and the Borghetto Santo Spirito dance hall, while Christmas-New Year and Easter holidays were dedicated to Cafe Roma because vacationers returned.

Working and studying without ever having a break was very demanding.

I was young and healthy, so I survived!

I graduated in July 1964 and was very happy, as were my parents.

As I said, between 1964 and 1968, the economy had entered a recessionary phase with repercussions on new jobs.

That season I continued to work at Cafe Roma, only in the evening, while during the day I had found a job as a mechanical tracer at Salimbeni mechanical workshop in Albenga. It was a very tough job because we handled iron profiles by hand and had to "rivet" and drill them to build automatic greenhouses for vegetables. Clearly. It wasn't my job, and there were more hammer blows hitting my nails than those hitting the rivet.

But at least for that summer, having two jobs, one during the day and one at night, I managed to make ends meet sufficiently well.

The problem was in winter or after the season had closed.

However, 1965 was also fortunate. On one hand, I enrolled at the University of Genoa in the Physics faculty, and on the other, I found a job as a teacher at the E. Fermi institute in Albenga under Prof. Aldo Boazzo, who later became a great supporter and friend.

I taught daytime Physics to accounting students, general culture for the secretarial course, and finally technology and mechanical drawing for the evening classes.

At the same time, I did my best to attend Physics classes with my inseparable friend Dario Braggio.

I continued to apply for jobs in industry in Piedmont and the Milan area. I absolutely wanted to work as an expert in a company.

Fiat and Olivetti were in my sights, as were Montecatini and other industries in the North-West.

But nobody called for an interview.

Once, ironically, I was recommended by Don Lasagna to Olivetti.

One fine day, after sending yet another job application, I was called to Ivrea for an interview, for which I arrived perfectly on time after an 8-hour train journey.

The interview was going quite well when suddenly a phone call arrived. My interviewer stopped, looked at me, and answering the phone said: "Dear Don Lasagna, your recommended candidate is in front of me right now and isn't doing badly, unfortunately, due to this phone call of yours, Olivetti not accepting recommendations, I am forced to discard him."

The interview ended there.

And from then on, I understood the meaning of the phrase that luck is blind, but bad luck sees perfectly well!

For some years I had a girlfriend (the one with the green eyes) whom I loved very much. Our story began when we were just a little more than teenagers and lasted for five years.

Not everything went smoothly, mainly due to my social status, which was judged insufficient by her mother, while her father, a splendid person, understood that I was working hard to build a future.

At that time, unlike today, relationships between fiancés were almost always chaste because the girl had to be respected until marriage.

Our relationship was only and exclusively platonic. Today this is inconceivable!! But back then, it was like that.

And perhaps I still remember it because it was like that!

In small towns, this was respected, but clearly, it was a problem for us boys to remain chaste.

This was especially true if you worked the seasons like me in Alassio, where temptations came from all sides, especially from older women looking for young boys. Just like now. Not much has changed, right?

We boys indulged... oh yes.

Those kinds of relationships were open, didn't require any commitment, and gave us experience.

However, it will be difficult to understand, but we never stopped loving our real girlfriends.

Absurd? Perhaps, but it was truly so!

These (summer) betrayals, purely based on 'whoever I catch, I catch' type adventures, bothered our local girlfriends quite a bit. But for the boys, the word 'chastity' was hard to pronounce.

The real girls were for winter, a little less for summer. That was how it was for me too. Unfortunately, one day I discovered that girls also knew how to look around, and my girlfriend was also seeing someone else, who I later learned she married.

I was also stubborn and pig-headed like a mule.

I selfishly got very angry and decided to do without her.

In reality, I never understood if it was she who had decided she could do without me!

Yes. I think that's exactly how it was.

An attempt at reconciliation was made, but nothing could make me change my mind, and I decided it would be over forever. I remember the last meeting in the square of the Croce Bianca in Albenga, and then I never saw her again. I only discreetly inquired about her from a distance, but nothing more.

That relationship marked me for the rest of my life.

I was very bitter about my social position, which was not deemed adequate by her mother.

You won't believe it, but for a long time, I fought, I did the impossible to improve my position precisely to show her that she was wrong and that in the end, I would succeed in improving myself.

I believe this is the secret basis of my success for what it has been.

I could write an entire book about this youthful love. This would be full of those beautiful feelings that are rarely found today.

Such feelings accompanied me for a long time.

The questions like 'what if' lasted for a long time, but then it all passed. Time is a great healer.

In my heart, I wished her much happiness, and as far as I know, her life has been happy.

During that moment of bitterness, one Sunday, by chance, a beautiful young lady, in Alassio, at the bus stop, asked me if I could give her a ride as she had missed the bus that was supposed to take her to work in Albenga. The young lady was an employee at the then Stet telephone company, which later became SIP and today is Telecom Italia.

The same evening, at the time of her return to Alassio, I showed up again at the bus stop and gave her a ride back.

We started dating regularly without any commitment from either side.

I just needed to heal my wounds. She listened patiently and gave me good advice.

Erminia, that was her name, despite being 41, was a beautiful woman (she strongly resembled the actress Lia

Zoppelli). I really enjoyed going out with her.

During our meetings, I told her about my life story and recent disappointment. Erminia was very understanding; she listened to me, advised me, and never forced the situation in one direction or another.

I continued to attend university in Genoa.

One fine day, we realized we loved each other with a beautiful and crazy love (or at least judged so by most due to the age difference).

Seven months after we met, we spent a vacation on Lake Maggiore, and it was there that Erminia told me that the relationship as it was set up had to end.

I then asked what she would say if I asked her to marry me? She cried, perhaps from joy, perhaps from surprise, she didn't answer me immediately.

However, I didn't yet have the means to support a family, being a working student.

She made me reflect on the age difference. But that didn't matter to me at all.

My desire to marry her was strong, so I started actively applying for jobs at companies in the North.

That woman brought me luck.

As if by magic, one evening after talking to her on the phone, I found a copy of the Corriere della Sera newspaper on a table at the student house of the University of Genoa, which had an advertisement stating that SGS-Fairchild was looking for a chemical expert for their research laboratory in solid-state physics and for high-vacuum applications. On impulse, I grabbed a pen and paper, invented a resume, and requested an interview.

Yes, but what the heck was I supposed to know to work at SGS-Fairchild if I didn't even know what they produced? A colleague who had studied electronics told me they made Semiconductors. Semiconductors? Never heard of them. Someone explained to me that a diode or a transistor are semiconductors (I only knew about Japanese transistor radios because my friends from Garlenda had given me one as a graduation gift).

Having to face an interview and appear intelligent, I did the smartest thing I could: I went to the library, researched this technology as best as possible, and was recommended the Italian text considered the Bible of that nascent technology at the time. The text was by Prof. Bolognesi and said everything that was known then about the chemistry of Silicon and the fabrication of semiconductors.

Without knowing if I would actually be called for an interview, I plunged into reading the book, asked study colleagues for explanations of what I didn't understand, and after a month, I had finished my preparation.

The technology was truly very complex, and making a semiconductor required complex chemical-physical processes and very expensive equipment.

I told all this to Erminia on the phone, and she, who believed in me, said: "Don't worry, this is the good time." And so it was. Soon after, SGS-Fairchild called me for a general interview, which I passed well, then immediately

a technical interview which 33 candidates participated in (almost a state competition).

I ranked first and was hired on May 19, 1967. My first salary was 90,000 Lire per month (half of what I earned at Cafe Roma if I included tips).

Recently, I reconnected with the people who hired me, and together we pleasantly recalled the moments and details of that interview.

But finally, I was taking the first step towards what I had set out to do. I had opportunities to seize, and I had to and wanted to demonstrate what I would be capable of.

The bet with myself didn't start then, but the new resolution I made lasted for my entire working life. Totò used to say that in a man's life, the exams never end. Very true!

In my life, I have faced many.

I remember the day I left the interview with the hiring letter in hand, I called Erminia and, crying with joy, said: "Thank you for your trust, and if you wish, we will get married soon." I continued: "Only a very courageous person could bet on a 23-year-old

who has just got a job like me." I knew that Erminia had faith in me and our future and that in the end she would be convinced that marrying me would be the right thing for us, even if we would have to fight against age prejudices.

I was very young, but I was sure of one thing: my ability to gauge people I met at first glance. This very valuable experience was acquired by meeting thousands of people at Cafe Roma. It was a window on the world, and if you observed carefully, it wasn't difficult to get to know people upon the first meeting.

Good intuition comes from sniffing a lot!

After being confirmed in my job, we decided that we would get married in November.

I remember the moment I introduced Erminia to my mother and father. It was a much-dreaded moment.

A 19-year difference is not easy for parents to swallow!

It was night, and my parents were fishing for mullets with a rod in the small port of Alassio. I knew exactly where

they were, and we approached with soft steps. Erminia, once there, said "Good evening" with a beautiful voice tone that only she had.

My father turned around and smiled broadly at that voice. With him, I understood it was done. It wasn't the same for my mother. After the introductions and without beating around the bush, we communicated our decision to marry on November 4th. It was then around mid-October, and we were on the time limit to get the necessary publications in the town hall and in the church.

Once at home, my mother tried with all her might to dissuade me, but her efforts were in vain, and she finally accepted reluctantly. The reason she gave was the big age difference. Nothing else to object to.

I have always been very stubborn and have always trusted my great intuition, and I have absolutely always done what I decided to do with my life without any regrets.

Financially, we could count on a loan from my parents, some of my savings, Erminia's contribution, and my and her employee salaries. We thus judged that it was feasibleto set up a home.

Again, despite many rowing against our decision, I decided to marry Erminia and did so as promised on November 4, 1967.

I was a little over 23 years old. Portofino, Pisa, and then headed towards Rome on our honeymoon in a Fiat 500.

Precisely...driving on the Autostrada del Sole (highway) near Attigliano, the car suddenly stopped.

I had no idea what had happened.

It was freezing cold, I waited for someone to pass to ask for help, but no one passed for a long time. The Autostrada del Sole was not as busy as it is today!

Finally, in the opposite lane, I saw the blue lights of the traffic police, and with a flashlight in hand, I gestured to make them stop.

They came towards us, climbing over the guardrail, and called the tow truck.

We were transported with the car to a garage in the small town.

The mechanic explained that the timing chain had broken and that he could only repair it the next morning.

Great blow!

We asked where we could spend the night and were told there wasn't a hotel nearby but he would ask if they would host us for the night.

And so it was; and so I understood that not all troubles come to harm.

That evening, our hosts not only accommodated us but also invited us to have dinner with them.

At that time, families trusted even strangers much more.

We were guests of a family of four: father, mother, and two little daughters.

It was immediately clear they were a decent family. The kind and loving glances they exchanged with each other were the best identity card to represent them.

During the conversation, we talked about ourselves and our honeymoon. Then, talking about where we would settle down, we said it was problematic to know where, as Erminia was to be transferred to Milan, but the issue was when that would be possible.

The advantage of working in the national telephone company was that practically in every city there was an office with at least one employee where theoretically a transfer would have been possible, while the disadvantage was that the enormous dimensions and elephantine structures would take a long time to examine our case, with the possibility of it taking at least a year.

Being newly married and already knowing we would have to live, I in Milan and Erminia in Alassio, and meet once a week was not the peak of our aspirations!

The gentleman, named Romeo, listened attentively to our story and I noticed he had a smile on his lips.

Typical of someone who knows more than they let on!

At a certain point, he asked us if he could help us settle Erminia's transfer case, and we replied that we would certainly greatly appreciate any help that could facilitate the transfer.

Romeo took paper and pen, noted down all the details, and told us he would do his best.

The next morning, Romeo accompanied us to the garage to pick up the 500, and then we continued to Rome.

It was a short but intense honeymoon. It was my first visit to the capital and its immeasurable beauty and historical, artistic, and religious value.

I was very excited to be in the city that was the capital of the world!

We visited St. Peter's, the eternal city, and, as protocol dictated, the Vatican and its beautiful museums.

I remember being very impressed by the frescoes in the Sistine Chapel, especially Michelangelo's Creation.

Those two fingers touching, passing life from one to the other, say much more than any possible description.

They were very happy days, but with the worry of having to set up home upon returning.

Could you get married without having a fixed abode? Well, yes, we had!

God helps the bold and the crazy!

On our way back, we visited Florence. It was the year after the Arno flood of 1966. The damage caused by the water was still clearly visible, especially along the Arno, and unfortunately, many people were left homeless, and many works of art of inestimable value were damaged, irreparably lost, or damaged.

We headed towards Milan where we planned to stay at a guesthouse for a few days and then have Erminia return to work in Albenga and me to Agrate Brianza.

From time to time we stopped to call home (at that time mobile phones were not yet imaginable, we used coin-operated phones!). During a stop in Piacenza we called my mother-in-law in Alassio and she told us that a certain Romeo had asked about us as he needed to speak with us urgently.

We called him at the number he had left and with immense pleasure he informed us that he had discussed our case with a highly placed person he knew and that Erminia's transfer request had been accepted! And that we would have to go to the SIP office in Milan, Via Parini, the next day to arrange the details of the transfer!

Not all evil comes to harm!! It was truly true... if the car hadn't broken down... and we hadn't been lucky..!

We never stopped thanking Romeo, who told us he was very happy to have been able to help us.

We spoke again but never met him again. He was an angel who disappeared into nothingness. Thank you, Romeo, thank you very much.

Erminia went to the office and was informed that she would be transferred to that office on Via Parini at the beginning of December. Was it a change of wind?

I think it certainly was. That same afternoon we decided to look for a house; it was pouring rain, but the weather didn't stop us.

We decided to look in the vicinity of Piazzale Loreto as the location would be convenient for Erminia's work, as tram 38 passed right by, and for mine, as I could easily take Viale Palmanova and thus head towards Agrate Brianza.

Unimaginable today, we found a vacant three-room apartment on the seventh floor of Via dei Transiti. That same afternoon, we paid the deposit and signed the contract.

The next day, with the house floor plan in hand, we were in Lissone choosing and ordering furniture.

Getting married, moving, and finding a house in ten days... this is called... well, you know... having... luck.

Our marriage lasted 19 years.

It was a happy marriage, and we loved each other very much. However, the last 4 or 5 years were a bit challenging.

Erminia was about 60 years old, I was 41. She was retired. I was in the prime of my career.

We realized that our love story was coming to an end because our ways of planning our future were totally different. Hers was that of someone who had arrived, mine was still in full swing.

She would have wanted me always close, while I was traveling around the world for work.

The gap was widening and pushing us too far apart.

But until then?

It had been a beautiful period. In the beginning, full of difficulties, including financial ones, which gradually resolved themselves.

Erminia was for me a wife, a lover, and a mother in the true sense of the word. I would do it all again, even knowing that (as it effectively happened) one day we would separate.

Our love story ended, but not the mutual respect, esteem, and affection of people who shared a good part of life together, loving each other.

Erminia is no longer in this world, she left us in May 2005.

Together with my second and current wife Fiorella (whom she greatly esteemed), we suffered greatly from her passing, aware that a fixed point in my life had left me forever.

It was very beautiful when, before getting married, I went with my future wife to introduce her. Erminia looked at her, caressed her face gently and said: "Make him happy, he deserves it, he is a good man. I loved him but the age... divided us." Thus Erminia blessed our wedding.

The career in the Company.

Semiconductor technology was in its early stages. People were starting to talk about integrated circuits like DTL, TTL, and so on. I worked in R&D in the group of Dr. Armando Bottelli and Franco Marcantonini, and I was involved in experiments for depositing thin films under high vacuum for interconnecting the various parts of the electronic circuit built on silicon, and also dielectric material made using cathodic sputtering or electron guns.

We were already capable of depositing controlled thicknesses of Aluminum, gold, silicon, and silicon dioxide of a few thousand angstroms.

In our group, we had great people who later became important, including Professor Federico Faggin, who invented the first microprocessor that changed the history of PCs: the Z80 and its series.

Federico was an electronic circuit designer. He was my desk neighbor for some time. One day he told us he had to go to Fairchild in the USA (our parent company) for a training course. Since then, I have only seen him in magazines and on TV. I have read a lot about him, but I have never met him again.

It is said that once in the USA, after some time, after designing for Intel, he designed the Z80 microprocessor and with this, he went to a bank to present it, and from this he came out with a financing of 300 million US Dollars (at that time and not only, it was a lot of money) with which he developed the microprocessor, founding Zilog. Is it not perhaps my luck to have met such a talented man?

Even today he is considered a guru of electronic design; he has been received multiple times by the President of the United States Obama for the awarding of honors.

In short, a very VIP person.

I, on the other hand, remained at SGS. My salary increased slowly. Researchers, then as now, were poorly paid. The experience I was gaining, however, was very valuable.

One day I saw in the newspaper that a company, Ates, also an electronic components company, was looking for a position that perfectly matched my specialization.

I replied, and after an interview with the then Engineer Paletto, with an office in via Gattamelat a in Milan, they immediately gave me a hiring letter with an economic proposal to double my salary.

It was the end of 1969. I went to the company and submitted my resignation to my then managers, who asked me why I wanted to leave. My answer was very sincere: my salary wasn't enough, and if it hadn't been for my wife Erminia's salary, who had transferred to Milan in the meantime, I would have starved.

My boss Armando told me he didn't want to lose me. He asked for a few hours before accepting the resignation and went up to the personnel office.

After a couple of hours, he called me at my desk and told me that the company not only offered me the competitor's salary but also added another 5%.

I asked when it would take effect and he replied from the beginning of the next month. I then asked if the proposal would be confirmed in writing and he replied that it was impossible not to create precedents.

At that point I remembered the old saying, well present in the minds of the farmers of the Garlenda valley, which states: What cannot be written cannot even be promised.

I picked up the phone saying that I would only accept if I received the confirmation letter by 5:30 in the evening, otherwise the resignation would be irrevocable.

I was aware of the important decision I was about to make and I was aware that it would be extremely difficult to find a work environment, modern, highly technological, in an American style, like SGS-Fairchild, but the needs of a young man who had started a family were many, including the psychological ones, as I was unhappy that my wife earned more than me.

My bad Ligurian mentality! What can I do? I'm made like that!

At 5:29 PM, they delivered the long-awaited confirmation letter of what had been orally promised, and I remained with the company until 1981.

That was an important step, not only for the money, but also because the company, in that brief period of time, to justify the significant salary increase, was forced to carry out an evaluation of my work and my potential. I came out of it very well, and this evaluation was then constantly taken into account throughout my career in the company and greatly facilitated my progress.

In the meantime, the company changed its shareholding structure three times, up to the current STMicroelectronics.

At the end of '69, R&D was transferred to Settimo Milanese, and I chose then to stay in Agrate and (another stroke of intuition) to transfer to the factory where a new experimental department for the production of digital integrated circuits DTL and TTL was starting up.

Management later chose me as department head. I was 27 years old.

During that period, I had the opportunity to learn the best about planning very complex productions from an American named Richard Catero who came from RCA, and from Adriano Servini, a young Anglo-Italian who knew a lot. I immediately understood that I had to pay close attention to the knowledge of these two people, as learning the science of planning well, combined with technological knowledge, productivity, cost control, and achieving goals, was the great secret of the success of American industrial productions.

Other former colleagues from whom I learned a lot are Auretta Cuccia and Giorgio Potenza. Both physics graduates, very good. They too would later have brilliant careers in this company.

The new department, which was supposed to emulate what Motorola did in the USA, very expensive for those times, with all American and Japanese state-of-the-art equipment, was now completed. The company had transferred factory personnel with some production experience from other departments.

I interviewed all the people and realized that my colleagues did not transfer what they considered to be the most potentially skilled people to me.

The matter was serious because the company's expectations for that department were very high. The future of the company depended on them, as indeed it did.

After consulting with Giorgio and Auretta, we decided to do something unique in the history of high-tech production.

We decided, before anything else, to bring all the workers, mainly girls aged about 16-19, with at best a middle school education, into the classroom for a month and explain to them the principles of semiconductor theory and of the Silicon used in the fabrication of semiconductors and therefore integrated circuits.

The handouts and lessons were based on explaining dipoles using green beans rotating on themselves, pots of beans boiling at different temperatures depending on whether they were located by the sea or on top of Mont Blanc, and other very beautiful examples that remained impressed on the minds of the trainees.

The course had tremendous interest, and finally, our girls knew what they were manufacturing, with what technology, the importance, and the attention they needed to pay.

This work group later became very famous, and even today (meeting some of them), they are proud to have been part of the pioneering department of this fundamental technology, protagonist of our modern era.

What would we do without PCs, mobile phones, TVs, and everything else, all based on electronics and thus integrated circuit chips?

During that period, I met several people who became my collaborators and were of vital importance for the success of the project called Module 1.

Module 1 because other departments would follow.

The first important person I met was Giuseppe Pozzi, known as Peppino.

A golden boy. A Bergamasco from head to toe.

Before joining our company, he worked at Falk and shoveled flux in blast furnaces. He had a middle school education. But he was an ace of intelligence who later, during his working period, graduated in industrial chemistry.

I appointed him as my assistant and production manager.

Together, we started production on a single shift, and the processes were started step by step with the help of an army of engineers.

Imagine that the processing of devices on silicon wafers lasted more than 40 days from start to finish. The worst enemy was dust. All treatments were and still are carried out in a totally aseptic environment with temperature and humidity controlled to the degree Celsius and within 5% of ambient humidity (these were very stringent parameters at the time).

All chemical reagents and materials used in processing are and were absolutely pure with contamination of external material tolerated at most a few parts per million!

Everything was going well when unfortunately a serious unforeseen event occurred.

On the evening of April 2, 1971, at nine o'clock, the security service called me to inform me that a fire had broken out in the new department on a PVC (Polyvinyl Chloride) washing hood.

I asked if there had been any harm to people, even though I knew that no one was supposed to be in the department during the night. Fortunately, I was informed that the damage was only material but extensive.

I went to the site and immediately perceived, even from a distance, the acrid smell typical of carbonized

PVC. PVC is a material that doesn't ignite, it only carbonizes, but during this process, unfortunately, it releases gaseous Hydrochloric acid which deposits on all surfaces and, if metallic, corrodes them and reduces everything to a mass of rust.

The analysis carried out afterwards pointed to human error and the lack of thermal safeties that would prevent a hot plate from reaching 900 C and thus melting the material.

We had all worked hard, and we realized that in a few minutes, all our efforts and investments vanished. All the people were left without a department and therefore without work.

We remained in total limbo for a few days until our then president, Ing. R. Bonifacio, president of the company, gathered us together, became aware of the investigations carried out that clarified what had happened, and informed us that everything had to be redone from scratch because without this experiment, the company would have no future.

We all worked day and night throughout the summer to save and recover as much as possible.

In October, the reordered new equipment arrived, and all together we finally began to restart production.

I remember that the only breakdown I ever had in my life occurred during that period, and I only recovered when I saw my department resume work.

After that, things went very well for several years. The results were excellent, and the department, as new technologies advanced, adapted to the new needs, producing Digital, Linear, Mos, CMOS circuits, and some microprocessors.

Based on the experience of Module 1, other new departments were started, and gradually SGS-Fairchild, the company became SGS, then SGS-ATES through a merger with ATES, a publicly owned company. Finally, it became SGS-Thomson by merging with the French public group, and now it is known as STM, STMicroelectronics.

This fine company has come a long way.

I remember that in 1981 the Italian group had a turnover of 400 million US dollars, today the group has a turnover of 9 billion and ranks 5th in the world ranking of semiconductor manufacturers, just behind giants like Intel and a few others.

But nothing happens by chance. And it's not free.

The major turning point occurred in 1979 with the arrival at the company's top management of a now very well-known name, Eng. Pasquale Pistorio.

I met him for the first time a few days after his arrival.

Nobody knew what he looked like until then. It was known that he was tough, pure Sicilian blood, and that he had been Vice President of Motorola USA and Europe. A role, if I remember correctly, spanning the two continents.

That morning, at eight o'clock, I received a call from the Ing. Pistorio's assistant, Mrs. Rosi, who wanted to speak to me. My legs started to tremble... The fact that Eng. Pistorio was dealing with me at eight in the morning could not be an indication of any good news.

I was wrong.

Without much preamble, he told me that around seven o'clock he had gone to the department to visit it and a certain Pozzi literally grabbed him by the lapels and threw him out because he was not wearing the necessary aseptic and safety clothing.

To myself I thought: the usual Pozzi, and without realizing it I started to justify him by the fact that no one until that time knew that it was Pistorio.

He cut me short and told me that Pozzi had done his duty very well and to consider him for a merit note.

He said goodbye and hung up the phone.

I was amazed and couldn't believe my ears. The CEO gets thrown out of a department and rewards the one who did it? This was unimaginable in the Italian culture I knew.

I had met an extraordinary person with whom I had the opportunity to collaborate, although I never reported directly to him in the years to come.

Pistorio achieved in 25 years of activity what he had promised during the first meeting with all the staff in Agrate.

STM surpassed almost all its competitors in the sector and particularly the Motorola semiconductor division. The promises made way back in 1980 were all fulfilled and went well beyond expectations.

He is an icon for all of us.

To understand his way of managing and motivating his collaborators, I say the following: he once sent me a manuscript in which he congratulated me for certain historical results achieved in production, asking me what

he could do to thank the entire team of workers and supervisors.

I ventured to suggest that he could offer a lunch to the entire staff with his presence.

Within 1 minute he accepted and two days later the entire team of 100 people were transported by bus to Sant Eustorgio, a very famous restaurant in Arcore.

It was a memorable and cordial lunch, Pistorio joked with the entire group, which was predominantly made up of young female workers.

Later I asked someone if they might have preferred a salary increase instead of the lunch offered by Pistorio. Everyone replied that having an invitation from Pistorio was the highest recognition for them, and so it was for me too.

The STM management team, in addition to Pasquale Pistorio, consisted of great names, some of whom are now retired. It is difficult to name them all, but one person very dear to me whom I wish to mention is Engineer Paletto, who dedicated his entire existence to this company.

I left STM in Agrate Brianza for the first time in 1981 to found a company with American capital, Hunt Chemicals, which was involved in the commercialization of chemicals for micro and macro photographic image reproduction.

I returned in January 1984 at the invitation of Engineer Pistorio and my direct boss Dr. Giancarlo Bedendo.

My task was to take back the management of production and the process support engineering group, and at the same time train new managers within the group from recently hired young graduates.

You will probably wonder why I mention so many names that are almost unknown to everyone, the answer is that I don't want them not to have a place in my story and that they remain there as long as this writing remains.

I believe mine is an inner necessity that also aims to thank all these people who have been part of my life story.

Indeed, I returned to SGS and performed the task for two years, then by a gentlemen's agreement I returned to Hunt Chemical, which later became Olin Hunt, then Olin Ciba Geigy (OCG), then Olin Microelectronic Materials, and finally Fuji Microelectronic Materials.

The company name changed many times, but the business and high-tech products always remained strategically important and very advanced.

With my entry into Hunt Chemical, my job became that of a supplier, even to the company of which I had previously been an executive. My production life therefore ended for the first time in 1981 and definitively at the end of 1985.

I was 37 years old, in the prime of my career, and in a flash, I decided to change my life again.

Here below I tell you how.

During the STM years and the start-up of the Module 1 department, I met a person who later completely changed my life.

This gentleman named Pierre was our supplier of a highly scientific material called photoresist. Without it, the process of transferring the micro image onto the circuit created in silicon would have been impossible.

Those in the know will probably shudder at the simple terms I use in this writing. But if I didn't, very few people would understand what I am writing about.

Pierre is of Swiss origin with Italian maternal roots.

He spoke appropriate Italian but with the typical Franco-German-Italian accent.

Pierre, as I said, was our interface as a seller and also provided technical assistance when the problems to be solved were not too complex.

He visited us about once a month for about half an hour and then returned to Milan to then go back to his base in Belgium.

Pierre was a thin and tall man, about two meters tall, and he couldn't go unnoticed.

He was very polite (in a Swiss way), I rarely saw him angry, but the few times he was, he made it very clear.

Normally, important suppliers sometimes invited us to lunch or dinner; Pierre did not, he had never done so, thus maintaining the appropriate distance between client and supplier.

At that time, a serious technical problem arose related to a brand new material which unfortunately (we discovered much later) was sensitive to ozone.

Ozone is oxygen O3 instead of O2 and is generated during thunderstorms, by the effect of electrical discharges or in the presence of car exhaust emissions.

In summer, the Brianza area experiences strong thunderstorms with electrical discharges, and moreover, the department overlooked the old track of the Milan-Venice highway, thus suffering from exhaust gas emissions that damaged our processing.

A bomb for our products!

To try to solve this problem, Pierre and my process engineering team worked day and night for over two weeks.

It was then that I had some very important exchanges of ideas with Pierre about life, about how to do business, and much more. We had become almost friends. But the necessary detachment always remained.

The problem remained, and production had been almost blocked for 20 days now.

Pierre then, in a last-ditch effort to save the business, invited me and my engineering manager Ercole Stroppolo, who reported to me, to the research laboratory in Rhode Island where these products were developed and produced.

Thus, in the distant year of 1972, on the sixth of January, I set foot in the United States for the first time at Boston airport.

That winter was the worst in the USA in 20 years. Coming out of the airport at 9 in the evening, we found about one meter and twenty centimeters of snow and the temperature was -15 C.

That time I had proof that in New England, when it's cold, there are no half measures!

With Ercole Stroppolo, we met all the R&D designers at Hunt Chemicals, but unfortunately, we didn't get anywhere and I was forced to tell Pierre that he had lost our business for the time being.

The volume of business he was losing with us was very important for him, and we were therefore very worried about the effect on him personally and generally on his company.

Unfortunately, we had no choice but to change supplier. We switched to the competition, which had a less advanced but more stable product.

Pierre accompanied us to New York, where Ercole and I spent our first weekend. It was on that occasion that

Pierre told me that if they decided to open a company in Italy, he would ask me to be the founder.

Imagine: he had lost the business and he offered me a possible engagement!

Years passed, the problems were solved, and we bought products from this company again. In the meantime, Pierre had climbed the career ladder, becoming a VIP and General Manager Europe. And I no longer had direct contact with him.

Many discoveries were made in microelectronics, and semiconductor technology advanced at a crazy speed. Investments in the sector tripled every year. Equipment manufacturers had invested billions of dollars in both the USA and Japan.

New factories for the fabrication of silicon integrated circuits sprang up like mushrooms.

America and Japan were the masters of the market.

I went to the States many times to manage relationships with Fairchild and RCA to transfer production of new technologies such as Low power Schottky and CMOS silicon gate to Italy.

Both these technologies had a logic function with very low energy consumption. In short, they consumed very little, and the batteries that powered them began to last a long time.

Besides consumption, integration (how small the circuit could be made) was greater, and therefore more complex functions were possible per unit area of silicon!

In addition to the direct responsibility for the production departments, I also had the responsibility for process engineering, and with my group, besides dealing with the transfer of technologies from R&D or purchased from third parties, I was in charge of designing and equipping new production departments, including training of personnel who by then were always working on three daily shifts and 7 days a week.

My total work group consisted of about 500 people.

In reality, I was very satisfied, as I was well-placed and esteemed by my superiors, and everything suggested an excellent career within the group.

But, one evening in April 1981, ten years after visiting New York, I received an international call from a certain Mrs. Teresa from Belgium, who introduced herself as Pierre's assistant.

She essentially asked if I could meet Pierre at 9 PM at the Hotel Michelangelo in Milan.

In a fraction of a second, my mind realized that if Pierre wanted to meet me, it had some connection to the job offer he had made many years before.

I accepted the meeting and drove to the Hotel Michelangelo in my Lancia Beta Montecarlo.

This car, which I had bought second-hand from a wealthy cousin of Erminia's, was meant to redeem the bicycle and Vespa of my early years.

But that Vespa has never been replaced by anything, to the point that I still keep it.

While driving to meet Pierre, I prepared the speech to use in case Pierre did make a concrete job offer.

That evening with Pierre, for the first time since we had known each other, we had dinner out together at Da Cesare in Via Cenacolo in Milan.

During dinner, Pierre simply asked me if I remembered what he had told me in New York. I replied affirmatively.

Pierre used few words to tell me that he was asking me for a difficult thing that had no guarantee of success and that on the first day of work I wouldn't even have a desk to lean on.

In addition to products for microelectronics, in which I was certainly an expert, the company marketed three other lines: copier toners, photofinishing products for developing photographic film and paper, and then the second most important line dedicated to the printed circuit industry.

Essentially: zero offices, zero warehouses, zero collaborators.

Expectations very high.

Just what was needed!

I have always loved challenges, simple things without a challenge were not for me. So I opened my ears and started to be open-minded in my mind.

Salary: double what I earned at ST!

Annual bonus upon achieving results equal to salary...

I liked this aspect very much and so I was inclined to accept. On the other hand, I already knew a lot about this company, also in the USA, having visited it with Ercole 10 years earlier.

I only needed to visit the plant headquarters in Belgium and then I would be able to make a decision.

I asked Pierre if he could prepare a draft contract, but he replied that he did not intend to do so and that everything should be based on a mutual trust agreement, meaning on the given word. I knew Pierre and I knew that this was the act of trust he was asking of me to hire me. It was also the guarantee he wanted to demonstrate that I would give my best to achieve the company's objectives.

I went to Belgium and accepted the offer sight unseen. I only received the contract with my third salary!

This despite the fact that I realized I was moving from a job embedded in a large company with technical production characteristics to a predominantly technical commercial job. I had never sold anything except drinks at Cafe Roma!

And the new job presented major questions.

But, I had to bet on myself, and on September 1, 1981, I started the new job.

My new life outside of STM.

The first episode I love to recount relates to the job interview I had in Belgium with Pierre.

I arrived at Brussels airport in the afternoon, and a car was waiting for me at arrivals to take me to Hunt Chemicals.

Once in Pierre's office, we had a coffee, and he took me to visit the plant.

It certainly wasn't the size of STM, but it was quite large for the type of chemical products manufactured there.

I was positively impressed.

So, 6 PM arrived, and there was no talk of work in personal terms. Pierre told me that we would go to dinner with his then-partner, Florence.

We stopped by his house to pick up Florence, and we went with his Porsche Carrera 911 (in reality it was the company car, lucky him!). I moved to the back seat and noted during the short journey that in that position, the car was quite uncomfortable, almost as uncomfortable as my Beta Montecarlo, and the back seat couldn't even accommodate my briefcase.

Florence was listening intently to what we were discussing. But still, Pierre didn't talk about work.

It was strange, but Pierre was a very original person.

After dinner, they asked me if I would agree to go for a drink at a very famous nightclub in Brussels. I accepted very willingly.

So I entered the Show Point in Place Stephanie for the first time. A fabulous nightclub where they had cabaret shows, but especially stripteases by dreamlike girls. There were many girls, young, scantily dressed, and beautiful. Pierre and Florence knew them and greeted them with a kiss, one by one, and they reciprocated.

That evening was very nice for me. We drank good brand champagne all night, I chatted with beautiful girls and completely forgot the purpose of my visit. Florence did everything to make me feel comfortable and I felt as if I was born into that environment.

The experience from Cafe Roma, although very different, came in handy in that case.

We left the club at six in the morning. Pierre said goodbye with a "see you soon in Milan". At that point I asked him: "what about the interview?"

He replied laughing: "You just successfully completed it," and added, "I know Giuliano at work, what I didn't know was Giuliano in life, and tonight I got to know him. A person who, after traveling all day to get here, is able to stay sober and chat amicably with people all night, this person is the one I'm looking for." He was looking for an honest person who loved life, who enjoyed earning well and was ambitious to always do better. I was that person, I proved it that evening.

Needless to say, I was hired.

One should not be deceived by Pierre's behavior, as he was also what he looked for in his collaborators, namely fast, concise, and decisive.

I started my job on September 1, 1981, looking around at nothing. So I started looking for a small office with two rooms, and warehouses of 1000 sq m approved for our chemical products.

I was lucky and found them immediately in Via Mecenate in Milan. But the luck of all lucks was when I met Maria Grazia. A girl who worked in accounting at CIT in Galleria Vittorio Emanuele. I remember meeting her at a mutual great friend's house, Lella from Garlenda, whom I have already mentioned. Talking with her, I immediately understood that this person was right for us. On intuition, I made her a very attractive offer, and since she was as crazy as me, she accepted and became my assistant for the rest of my corporate life.

She started working part-time with me when she still had to finish her notice period at CIT.

We ordered the office furniture, and finally, we decided to design the invoice form with pencil and ruler, then writing the various boxes with an electric Olivetti typewriter.

That invoice brought us luck, and we photocopied it for another two years.

We often had visits from foreign colleagues. The official language was English.

Colleagues had a great difficulty pronouncing the name Mariagrazia, so we decided to call her by a new name, Laura. Laura was easier for Americans and French speakers, who called her Lora.

Well, she remained Laura for the next 24 years!

I immediately focused on transferring the sales made until then for the semiconductor industry, in which I was an expert (STM was our largest Italian customer).

And subsequently, I focused on launching chemical products and printed circuit products.

The product expected to generate volume was a copper-ammonia etchant for etching copper traces on printed circuits. In Italy, there were many small industries producing printed electronic circuits, most of which were located in the Northwest, some in Marche, Tuscany, and Rome around Via Tiburtina. Then nothing else.

The territory was vast, but it would have been nothing if I had the list of companies. Nowadays, with the Internet, it would have been child's play. At that time, there were only yellow pages that gave an address, mapped where they were located, but said nothing about their size, what and how much they did, and so on.

Laura and I had all the lists region by region and created a small manual database.

We wrote a presentation letter and sent it to 200 addresses. No one ever decided to contact us spontaneously. I realized that launching this product line was the real reason the company had opened in Italy. Until then, the product was manufactured in Belgium and transported to all European countries in drums or tankers.

The etching product, once used, became enriched with copper salt up to almost 160 grams per liter, thus becoming a toxic product that had to be disposed of in compliance with all laws. The contained copper could in turn be recovered through a specific treatment and constituted a resource if properly treated.

The salts thus obtained had their own market for use, whose value abundantly covered the value of the fresh product we sold, the cost of transport to and from of the used product.

In Italy, there was a local competitor with a plant in the Turin area, who had a monopoly on this market and managed to offer competitive prices that we could never match.

We were losing on all fronts.

Time passed, and I wasn't making any progress. Anxiety began to set in.

I then decided to visit all the factory addresses region by region, door-to-door. I remember driving my car more than 60,000 kilometers in 5 months.

But in the end, I formed a clear idea. I spoke with Pierre, expressing my concern about not having acquired a new customer in the printed circuit industry in six months of activity. Fortunately, the products sold for microelectronics were doing very well. He very calmly told me to continue because I was doing well and eventually, the results would surely come. In the meantime, we were fortunate and capable of finalizing an agreement for the manufacturing and recovery with a Milanese chemical company, Caffaro

Spa, listed on the stock exchange, which guaranteed us competitive and innovative prices and services compared to the existing competition.

I remember that I started revisiting the customers one by one, region by region, armed with interesting ideas and proposals.

It was a lot of hard work, but I was young. Certainly, staying at ST wouldn't have been so physically demanding.

Finally (I remember it exactly), I visited a small company in the Bologna belt, ACE, which ordered

a few drums of product worth about 60,000 lire, to be paid with a bank receipt at 60 days!!

Wow!, I had made the first sale. I was happy and exhilarated as if I had won the football pools.

I called Laura on the phone and we congratulated each other.

That evening I called Pierre and he told me to go to the bar to celebrate. I drank a good bottle of Champagne costing 30,000 lire and went to bed happy as a lark.

That bottle brought good luck because within a year I took the product sales turnover from zero to over two billion lire and achieved a 60% Italian market share. And in 1982, believe me, for a two-person company, that was already an excellent turnover, which added to the microelectronics turnover of about 1 billion... things weren't going so badly!

We worked like crazy, but it was a great success and the company rewarded us for it.

Our business at the ST plant in Agrate and Catania was doing very well. We were able to always propose new products that kept pace with new technologies, and consequently, the turnover grew in proportion to the customer's growth.

Everything was going well, but the work wasn't finished. We still needed to launch the photographic chemical products business in the Italian market.

We hired more people in the office, Carla and later Silvia, reaching a total of about 15 people.

In 1997, we moved the offices and warehouses to a building in San Giuliano Milanese.

Dr. Michele and Dr. Stefano were also added to the microelectronics team.

I began studying the market when Pierre decided to hire a specialized salesman, Claudio, for the photographic division.

He reported organizationally directly to the Photo division and hierarchically to me in Italy. In other words, I had almost nothing to do with him.

Claudio lived in Rome and every week, even though he had accommodation in Milan, he drove home on weekends with the company car.

In one year I was told he had driven over 100,000 kilometers (all expensed and salaried). But not a drop of photographic product was sold.

Meanwhile, as I said above, I had returned to STM for a couple of years.

I was replaced at Hunt by two colleagues for the Printed Circuits division because the volume of business achieved was such that to increase it further required an investment in a technician and a salesperson.

The semiconductor part was entrusted to Philippe, who covered it from the Paris office. The Photo part remained uncovered because the roman colleague "was let go, as they say in America." "We let him go!".

Meaning, fired!

Two years had passed since I left SGS, and many things had already changed. My production responsibility covered half of the Agrate plant.

I had my hands full even without looking for more headaches. Moreover, in my group, I had a good number of young graduates who were to become the new management of the company's future. I believe we succeeded well in this goal, as after a few years, they all distinguished themselves (and to put it in Mario Berrino's words) proved to be good runners, placing themselves at the top management levels not only of STM but also at the highest levels of companies competing with STM, just like Cafe Roma. they were a training ground of knowledge and life that gave excellent preparation to those who wanted to draw upon it.

Truly excellent colleagues, I hold them all in my heart.

After the two years of the agreement made with the top management of STMicroelectronics, and just before the corporate merger with the French Thomson, I returned to Hunt Chemicals with the consent of both parties. I realized then that I was no longer suited to being confined to a plant for my whole life. This was true even though STM offered opportunities for frequent travel to the United States and the Far East.

I felt the cage around me, and the job of sales manager better satisfied the expectations that had changed in me.

In a way, I had returned to my origins and to selling, not drinks or cocktails, but industrial products. I understood not long after that the art of selling, and especially organizing sales, is simply an art you either have or you don't, and it absolutely doesn't depend on what you sell but on how you sell it. This was the secret that Pierre had intuited while spending that month in close company in the production departments. He had understood it, I had not yet.

I returned to the company as the manager of the Italian branch.

I found all the serious problems again. Michele, an excellent colleague with a desire to work and a precision that always led him through all successes. The division in Italy reached sales of 40 million Dollars at its peak. Not bad, right? But this was after a few years and after the sale of a couple of important divisions. The global turnover would have been around seventy million dollars

or 100 billion old lire.

The problem of launching photographic products, our other product division, was right there in plain sight. The potential market was quite large back then. Digital photography, which timidly appeared around the 1990s, did not yet exist.

But Hunt Chemicals wasn't making any headway in the Italian market.

There was a lot to sell, but the market had to be conquered from giants like Kodak, Agfa, and the Japanese Fujifilm. Moreover, they sold the entire processing kit, from films to printing paper and products for developing and fixing the prints.

We only had products for developing and fixing, so we were very disadvantaged in our eyes and in the customer's eyes. Our products had gained a reputation in the market for being unstable. This was not actually true, as many small laboratory customers did not have the ability to perform those small quality controls on the baths and make the adjustments that chemically stabilized the developing baths, guaranteeing their quality and productivity over time, which everyone was already seeking then.

Unfortunately, all I knew about photography was the click of the camera shutter.

But I had a basic chemical background, so I could improve.

Pierre called me for a meeting in Belgium and without batting an eye, he told me that in addition to everything else, he was entrusting me with the launch of this division in Italy as well. He added that he was giving me carte blanche and was not placing any limit on the spending budget. On the other hand, within a year he wanted a 20% market share with a turnover of about two billion lire. Gulp!

I called Laura from Belgium, my conscience and my mentor, in addition to immense knowledge and a will of steel, and she told me, "If I know you well, you will succeed." The bets that seem already lost from the start stimulate you, so you will have fun. Start working. Well, the start was encouraging, already two people thought I would make it!

I returned home and began to think about what and where I needed to start to tackle this market.

At that time I talked a lot with Erminia, who listened to me very patiently.

She had a rare ability, synthesis; she could extract the needle from the haystack at first try.

Suddenly she said, "If I understand correctly, small laboratories have almost all technical difficulties, and being able to assist them would certainly be a plus." This, of course, provided that they start buying your chemical products. At that time, "Kiss un'ora Photo" mini-labs were starting to enter the market, competing directly with large laboratories that could deliver prints only after one or two days, with a certainly better average quality. But customers didn't care much, as they preferred to have the photos immediately. As for quality, it was considered good enough if, looking at the photo, customers saw themselves as beautiful and smiling. That was exactly how it was in 70% of cases.

How to make ourselves known, therefore reaching the customer by proposing the product-service combination with its relative added value?

At that time, a specialized periodical called Fotonotiziario was published in Italy, which published everything one needed to know about the world of photography. This periodical was followed by both photographers and laboratories as it was distributed capillarily to over 20,000 points. This periodical, like all periodicals, lived on advertising from major companies like Kodak, Agfa, and manufacturers of cameras and stores.

I then approached Aldo Muratore, a fellow Ligurian, who wrote for the periodical and also handled the commercial side, to find out what a large-scale advertising campaign would cost us. It turned out to be an incredible figure that I didn't feel I could spend, even though I had been given carte blanche on the budget.

During my talks with the commercial manager of Fotonotiziario, I learned that a very good editor of Greek-English origin, a certain Demetrios, had left the periodical and perhaps could help us with suggestions or anything else, given his deep knowledge of the Italian market. I met with him, we talked a lot, he listened to my strategy, and together we developed an attack tactic that I considered excellent. Demetrios also put me in touch with the head of the Color Color laboratory in Asti to see if he would be interested in teaming up with me to handle the assistance part. His name was Umberto Mezzetti.

Umberto was a Gentleman (with a capital G) who knew everything, absolutely everything, about the photographic process, and not only that, he was also a man with a heart as big as a transatlantic liner.

His thirty years of experience had begun in the laboratories in Ferrania, which later became 3M.

I made him such an interesting economic proposal that he could not refuse, and so the team was formed.

Now it was time to make ourselves known on the market and start selling.

We decided not to visit potential customers immediately and for three months only to work with Umberto and Demetrio on a mini-periodical that talked about the market (that was the part assigned to me, with lots of interviews and photos of me and Umberto on the front page). Just to be clear, I never wrote a single line myself. It was all the work of the editor-in-chief Demetrio and Umberto.

We decided to publish every 20 days with a print run of 2000 copies, all sent by mail to all photographic laboratories in the territory.

After the first two issues, customers who recognized themselves in the technical problems discussed, as they had those problems too, began calling Umberto to schedule a visit.

I'll make it short.

It was a landslide success. The chemistry sold itself through costumer’s active reference, sales increased visibly, Pierre's goal was surpassed. The following year, two more people were hired, a salesperson and a technical assistant to Umberto, Giorgio and Rambaldi, as Umberto could no longer cover the entire territory from the Alps to Sicily.

Laura from her desk smirked and made it clear "I told you so!"

I will end this beautiful story by saying that in the end we managed to sell six billion a year. A success of which we were all proud, Pierre the great boss, Paul the European head of the division.

To reward us, Laura offered me and Umberto a dinner, paying out of her own pocket!

Hunt Chemicals Italy and globally had reached the peak of success.

But alas, success attracts the attention of others, and so it was for us.

The Olin Co., an American group with a turnover of 2 billion Dollars, acquired the Electronics division, including printed circuits and Electronics.

Fujifilm, on the other hand, acquired the photographic products division along with the Belgian plant. Subsequently, the printed circuits division was also sold by Olin to McDermid.

The company was dismembered and sold division by division, and our hard work that had generated a large turnover was not rewarded. With the sales, all colleagues moved to the new companies. Laura, Michele, Carla,

Stefano, and I, the last ones remaining, felt a bit like those fathers and mothers who raise their children and then, after all their efforts, see them taken away. In short, we didn't comment, because it was unprofessional, but certainly in our hearts, we suffered tremendously. We consoled ourselves by saying... such is life!

For a couple of years, I was responsible in Italy for both Olin-Hunt and the new company created by Fuji called Fuji Hunt. This lasted for two years, then Fuji moved to a small town in Brianza with warehouses and offices, and at that point, we lost contact. It was the summer of 1992.

In the meantime, with the core business, a new company exclusively dedicated to microelectronics had been created, called OCG (Olin - Ciba Geigy), where both Ciba's business and the Olin business we managed had been consolidated.

In that year, Philippe, the French colleague who oversaw microelectronics in Italy during my absence at ST

(who had replaced Pierre and moved to Olin Co Europe), called me to lead the European sales group with the position of European Sales Director.

I had an office in Italy and one in Belgium and traveled in Europe and abroad for a total of 90% including weekends.

I spent my life in meetings, planes, and hotels. Sometimes I would wake up in the morning without remembering where I was at that moment.

It was also a disordered life with frequent dinners with clients and after-dinner meetings always with clients in some venue.

I frequented Scotland a lot where there were several important management clients in the company of the local manager Nick who covered Great Britain, the Scandinavian countries and Israel.

Germany with the then Siemens and other major clients followed by Herman and Franz.

France with Thierry and Jean Marie who followed the 4 ST plants plus another four important clients who required frequent contacts from me.

Italy with Michele and Stefano who accounted for the lion's share in terms of turnover.

Michele was able to acquire a significant amount of business from STM and achieve a market share in Italy of 80% with a large turnover.

Those were three very intense years for me, and my health suffered. In 1993, I was diagnosed with Type B Diabetes.

And I was no longer in peak condition. However, I held on until 2000.

In the same year, Philippe decided to restructure the company, also reorganizing sales in Europe.

I was appointed head of Southern Europe, taking direct control not only of France and Italy but also of Israel, India, and providing direct support to colleagues in Singapore regarding STM, which had and still has one of the largest semiconductor plants in the world in that state. In that support role, I was a customer's strategic worldwide manager.

In the years from 1992 to 2007 I often traveled to Asia, especially Singapore, Korea, Philippines, but also India and China, which in the meantime had grown enormously in the sector.

In Israel, we had two very important clients, one local and another who never wants to be mentioned but whom I can say is the world leader in microprocessors.

Business in that territory grew until 2005, then it intersected with the global crisis in the sector and a long phase of downsizing began. Among the beautiful things to remember about this wonderful land is the absolutely electrifying atmosphere one feels in the Church of the Holy Sepulcher and at the Wailing Wall at the base of the Walls of Solomon's Temple.

In those years I divorced Erminia who settled in Finale Ligure in an apartment I had bought some years earlier and where close relatives lived such as her sister, and her niece Giovanna.

Fiorella

I briefly mentioned my second wife Fiorella at the beginning of this writing, and I firmly believe that telling our story is a duty for me towards her and a pleasure for me to remember it in detail.

When I think about how our relationship began, I am reminded of what Manzoni wrote in I PromessiSposi (The Betrothed) in the chapter "Addio ai Monti" (Farewell to the Mountains) about Lucia, where he more or less quotes: "God never disturbs the happiness of men unless to provide a greater and more secure one."

In my case it was very true.

And like much of my life, instinct did the rest.

So I'll pick up with the meeting and how it happened with Fiorella.

In 1995 the first laptops appeared on the market. During a visit to Singapore I immediately bought one. The Internet for ordinary people was almost non-existent. I didn't have any provider, so it was my company that used IBM systems for the company, but nothing had been done to easily connect the various personal PCs and communicate with each other via email as is done nowadays.

With the total abandonment of paper supports. As I said, in my group I had a guy from Germany, Herman, who knew more about PCs and software than any of us. During a visit to his office in Munich, Bavaria, he showed me the internet connection he was using through a provider called Compuserve, which was very used in the USA, Germany, and Northern Europe. I was impressed and immediately subscribed to this provider personally.

I started to mess around with it, but clearly, I needed some help to start navigating effectively.

One afternoon I went to our accountant who provided our payroll service, and I saw the owner tinkering with his PC. I asked what he was doing, and a bit sheepishly he replied that he was chatting with some friends who were explaining to him that it was a good way to meet new friends.

This really piqued my curiosity.

I went closer and didn't miss the opportunity to learn the ABCs of navigation and the ABCs of chat.

Coincidentally, he also used Compuserve, and so, since I was already a bit familiar with the provider, it was easier than I could have imagined.

Once home, I took out my PC, connected it with the cable to the phone line, dialed the access number, and immediately found myself online. At that time, modems traveled at a speed of 10 KB per second. A slowness that would make you pale compared to the speed of our current lines of 1 gigabyte. To make a long story short, I found the forum I was interested in, entered, and it asked me what nickname I wanted to use. I chose Giuliano Milano so that my interlocutors would know where I was located.

So I entered this forum and saw a small window with a name on it, just one. Fiorella. Not knowing what to do and what it meant, out of habit rather than knowledge, I clicked a couple of times and a window opened where I understood I had to write something and send it to the other side of the wire. So I did, and timidly I wrote the word Ciao.

I understood absolutely nothing. I thought I had done everything wrong. Then suddenly, the reply "ciao" appeared; so it worked! What I had been told wasn't a lie.

I immediately asked Fiorella what she was doing all alone on this forum and she explained that there was a section where you could consult Italian recipes. I asked what was the need to consult them there when in Italy libraries were full of recipe books? she replied that in Italy yes, but not here in Washington DC where she lives, they were not found there, and so she had been informed of the existence of that forum. Strangely, she, like me, was connecting for the first time; to make a long story short, we chatted from 11 pm to 3 am. Then, having to close, I candidly asked for her phone number, saying, but without ulterior motives, that given my very frequent trips to America, if I were to pass through Washington, I would call her. Fiorella wrote down the number and I took note. We closed the chat with the promise to contact each other again.

Everything we had told each other in those hours of chat had impressed me sincerely because I had heard a true life story that had fascinated me and that seemed sincere. I, for my part, had been very sincere too, almost like in confession. The risk was minimal, who would ever meet? She in the USA and I in Milan?

I was intrigued by two facts, one by the spontaneity of the answers I received to my questions, the other was that she wrote perfect Italian.

We had said a lot, but certainly there was much more to say... the fact is that I had a strong urge to know if she had given me the number of the local cemetery instead of her home number.

I plucked up the courage, calculated that it wasn't deep night in Washington and estimated it was 10 pm.

I called.

A sweet voice in perfect Italian answered and said, "I bet you're Giuliano Milano," and I replied, a little timid and incredulous, "Ciao." Bet won.

We talked on the phone for another two hours. A costly call, but I felt it was worth it. We continued to call, chat, and exchange emails for the next two weeks. I felt I was falling in love with someone I had never seen, but whose character and thoughts were so close to mine that nothing else would matter, even if she were unattractive.

Since it was not possible to send photos attached to emails back then, I started to wonder if she would find me acceptable. I had always known my limits and never considered myself an Apollo. At best, I could be likeable and interesting, but certainly not a handsome man.

That June, I organized a worldwide sales meeting in Tenerife. The meeting lasted a week.

We worked hard. However, in my free time, instead of visiting the island with my colleagues, I mostly stayed in the hotel chatting with Fiorella.

It was in those days, just over a month after our encounter on the chat, that I learned I had to go to Rhode Island in the northern United States.

When it was time to describe ourselves, she described herself as light milk chocolate color because she was of Ethiopian mother and Italian Romagna father. Come to think of it, she also let slip a few words pronounced with a typical Romagna accent. When it was my turn to describe myself, I asked her if she liked Danny DeVito.

She laughed on the other end of the phone and asked why, do I resemble him? I replied that I was almost his double. It's true, a couple of times in New York at the Central Sheraton hotel, they mistook me for him.

I said I was short, chubby, and balding.

At this point, I thought... okay, now the line will click, and that will be the end of it!

I expected, therefore, a resounding hang-up. That didn't happen, also because the bill that arrived the following month was 300,000 lire for me and 400 dollars for her.

Skype didn't exist... damn it!

As I said, it so happened that I had to go to Rhode Island for a meeting that was being held there at the time.

Naturally, instead of arriving in Boston or New York, I took the long way around and landed just a little further south, in Washington D.C.!

Fiorella and I were happy to finally meet after almost two months of emails, chats, and phone calls.

The problem was how to recognize each other at the airport. It should be noted that photos via PC had not yet been invented, let alone webcams. Perhaps my self-description made things easier for Fiorella, but it wasn't so for me, as Washington airport was full of light chocolate-colored girls waiting at arrivals!

I disembarked and finally, after passport control, I picked up my suitcase, cleared customs, and stepped out into Washington Dulles airport for the first time.

A sea of people arranged in a V awaited at the exit of international flights, how would I find Fiorella? And if, once she saw me, she was disappointed and hid? A certain anxiety gripped my throat. I visualized everyone who was there waiting for someone and decided that

Fiorella was not among them. Why? I don't know, my instinct worked again.

So I headed quickly towards the taxi stand, dragging my suitcase with one hand and my very heavy briefcase full of work documents with the other.

At that time, there were some construction works at the airport, and for this reason, they had fenced off a passage, forcing everyone into a narrow corridor.

It was in that corridor that I glimpsed a splendid girl running towards the international arrivals entrance with the air of someone who was late. I observed her in astonishment and from her figure, which she had described, I decided she was Fiorella: and I called out: "Fiorella...?"

She stopped abruptly and ran towards me, threw her arms around my neck, and said, "Ciao Giuliano, welcome to me!"

She gave me the first real kiss and smeared lipstick all over my mouth and cheeks. I was happy about it. However, I must say that she has never lost the habit of smearing me with lipstick, even after a long time has passed.

We spent a few days together and finally had time to talk about everything about ourselves without being burdened by the costs of those damned phones and to get to know each other better.

After two days together, I left with the conviction that I had met the woman of my life.

This was the true beginning of our love story. Later, during subsequent trips to North America, I met her three children, Amanda, Travis, and Brian, from her first marriage to an American citizen.

Fiorella was then a flight attendant for Delta, and apart from the period we met, when she was home bound due to a car accident in a taxi in New York (where she was temporarily living for proximity to the airport) during a transfer from one terminal to another. Fiorella was a flight attendant, first for Pan Am and then for Delta Airlines, and often flew into Milan Malpensa.

She would arrive very early on Saturday morning and depart on Sunday around 8 AM. This gave us time to be together a bit and get to know each other better.

Her working weekend coincided with my weekly rest. I was actually living in Belgium for work reasons and returned every Friday. So everything had combined perfectly.

We could thus plan the subsequent steps, including our marriage.

We decided that she would move to Italy with all her children.

For this, I had to find a spacious house that would accommodate not only the new family but also my mother, who, after my father's death, had been living alone in Finale Ligure.

We found a house and planned to get married in Italy.

Unfortunately, we encountered the web of Italian bureaucracy, which at the time of obtaining the license at the town hall asked us for so many impossible documents to be presented by an American citizen, which Fiorella was and is.

She was born in Ethiopia to an Italian father and an Ethiopian mother.

The registry office official, seeing her American citizenship, asked for many documents very difficult to obtain, in order to admit us to the marriage.

It was then, in front of the registrar, that I asked Fiorella if it would perhaps be simpler to get married in the United States.

She replied that one month before the date you have to go to Court, make a sworn statement declaring that you are free from previous marital ties, cost 30 Dollars, and the thing is done.

Imagine what I decided to do in no more than two seconds? I told the official to forget about it, that we would get married in America.

So, a month later, on August 10, 1996, at the Marriott in Crystal City next to the Pentagon in Washington, we were happily married in a civil ceremony.

Only (on my part) my brother Piero and my sister-in-law Luciana could attend our wedding, plus Pierre and Philippe who arrived unexpectedly from Belgium.

While the other guests were all friends and relatives of Fiorella. Her mother Tayech joined us from Ethiopia. Her sister Piera and brother-in-law Giorgio, along with their daughters Carolina and Gaia, arrived from South Africa. It was a beautiful wedding, with many smiles and tears, as in the best tradition.

When we got married, Fiorella was 41, I was 52. The age difference that could have been a problem in the first marriage now turned against Fiorella.

15 years later, we love each other more than the first day. There is a perfect understanding and complicity between us that makes us always so happy.

Honestly, I must say that over time, our relationship has matured and continuously improved. I can say that now I understand what it means to be two bodies and one soul.

With Fiorella, we have learned to be well together even in total silence, certain of thinking simultaneously about what the other is thinking.

We have the same hobbies, we both love electronic gadgets, we build our own desktop personal computers, we love to travel; in short, we are very connected, similar and complementary in our relationship.

Sometimes I think that people who have known each other since kindergarten have never reached this level of understanding and symbiosis with each other.

But I must say that Fiorella also has a lot of patience..!

As of this date, 15 years have passed since our wedding, and our children, who were 14, 13, and 12 at the time, have now grown up.

Amanda, Fiorella's firstborn, is now thirty, graduated from high school in Virginia, and has given us a grandson, Jaiden, who was for me the joy given by God himself.

For family reasons Jaiden stayed with us in Italy for the first 5 years of his life.

Thanks to him, I was able to rejoice in the miracle of seeing a child grow up and helping to raise him.

That child whom I had always wanted so much to have but never did.

Jaiden filled this need of mine.

For these people, more than a grandchild, I consider him a son in all respects!

Travis, the second born, graduated in communication sciences, at George Mason University married a beautiful girl named Katiria, and they gave us two beautiful grandchildren, Nathan-Julian, and a granddaughter, named Adriana.

Travis is the perfect young man.

I always say that you could raise 10 young men like him all together!

He is precise, punctual, respectful, and everything good you can imagine in a young man.

And the other two? Yes, them too, but I must say, a little less!

Brian is the only son who stayed with us in Milan. He is 29 years old and unfortunately, like many young people today, struggles to find work and is therefore still dependent on us.

He doesn't even think about returning to America; he has integrated perfectly and is the most Italian in the family.

Fiorella and the whole family I married (yes, because I married an entire family) represent the emotional point of arrival in my life.

I have loved a lot, but I must say that I have never loved as I love Fiorella, aware of the values she represents for me.

My work, the final part, again.

Returning to describe the concluding part of the work, at the beginning of 1996, a tremendous opportunity arose with STMicroelectronics.

For a new plant in Catania, ST had asked chemical suppliers if they could provide a turnkey supply service for the purchase, storage, chemical analysis, and distribution of all chemicals needed in the processing of Integrated Circuits at the point of use. It was a new job for Europe and was called CMS, which in English we called "Chemicals Management Service," later renamed TCM or Total Chemical Management.

To put it briefly, it was a big deal.

In the USA, we already provided this service in the Phoenix, Arizona area, for ST and for Motorola and others.

In Italy too, we won the tender, and in addition to the normal activity, Laura and I threw ourselves into organizing things. She handled purchasing and material management, and I handled hiring (35 people), training, and startup.

It was what we had been seeking for a long time to redeem ourselves from the business divisions that had been sold in previous years.

I was working with the same enthusiasm as when we started Module 1 in Agrate.

American colleagues with experience flocked to help us, especially for the technical-management part of the chemical distribution room regarding the analysis laboratory.

Note that the analysis laboratory had the most sophisticated instruments, a mass spectrometers available on the world market.

The team had once again invented a new job. The hired personnel were all from Catania. I must say that despite the rumors I had heard, I found a team of guys so good and capable that it was difficult to find them in the

North; believe me, I have some experience with personnel!

In three months, the team was hired, trained, and started working to the client's satisfaction.

I remember the evening of the inauguration when we invited the top managers of STM Catania and Corporate. It was a splendid dinner with many toasts and photos. To our guys, it seemed impossible that such important managers as Ing. Laurent Bosson, Dr. Avallato, Ing. Rotondi, Dr. M. Mauri would sit at the table with them. From this, my team realized how important the new job was for STM and how much they expected from us.

This was something that truly motivated them very much for all the 10 years the team stayed together.

They did everything to satisfy the client. Note that the proper functioning of Factory M5 (Module 5) depended on them, which at the time employed about 1000 people and involved an investment close to 1.5 billion US$, recently inaugurated by Pasquale Pistorio and Romano Prodi, the then Prime Minister.

A ceremony to which, I say with pride, I was officially invited.

Not bad, right?

Well, these guys from Catania never failed once, and I assure you they gave their soul to create an opportunity to learn how to work in an international team like OLIN and then Arch Chemical. They succeeded very well and are now highly sought after.

When I hear it said that in that area there is no qualified and reliable personnel, I cannot help but react and recount my very positive experience with these guys.

All people, if well-motivated psychologically (but not only), will feel part of the good result they will be able to create and will always do their best to be esteemed by the work team they are part of and to be esteemed by the client and the boss.

To motivate them well, we hired the consultancy of an exceptional person, Dr. Nicoletti, a manager of Confindustria, who did an incredibly good job, especially on the concept of customer relationship and satisfaction.

What changed my way of seeing things was reading a small book.

It is very concise but full of truths that one almost thinks about during activity.

The title is "One Minute Manager". I don't remember if the English article 'the' was before 'One'.

I recommend reading it. It came out in Italy in 1985, and I hope it is still in circulation. I keep my copy together with the second volume, which was "One Minute Manager at Work".

This one is also very interesting, but certainly, in my opinion, not as good as the first book.

The thing that impressed me most about this manager, whose thoughts and actions are narrated, is that he had discovered a little secret.

Almost all bosses are very good at catching their collaborators when they make mistakes and therefore "scolding" them.

He explains that when you have to scold someone, you should do it for only one minute so that the person being scolded remembers the reason why they were scolded and not the way they were scolded.

The most important lesson I learned is the attention that bosses must pay to recognizing the positive results of an individual collaborator at the moment he is doing well. This is absolutely very motivating.

But the most important lesson was given to me by Pasquale Pistorio, who always told us to make sure your personnel participate in the final result and feel it as their own.

This new activity at ST in Catania greatly increased the business of Olin Hunt Italy and positively involved all 50 people employed in the company. The activity was very well appreciated by the client, and in 2000, we also obtained the CMS contract for the Agrate plant, R2, which constituted one of the two advanced semiconductor research poles worldwide.

Perhaps it is worth reminding those who do not know that STM had become enormous worldwide and had about 50,000 employees. With an annual turnover of about 9 billion US Dollars.

What an exceptional job Pistorio and his team accomplished in 20 years!

I swear that at the thought, I get emotional. Do you know why? Like my boys, I feel part of this result, having given something like 40 years of my working life.

Yes, in my small way, I contributed to the growth of this great and wonderful company.

Returning to CMS in Agrate, we obtained a five-year contract and redid everything that was done for Catania. There too, the client was very satisfied, and our 30 new guys on the team worked very hard. The Olin Hunt Italian division thus reached its peak in terms of turnover and company well-being. We were number 1 in Europe and accounted for more than 50% of the turnover.

Everything went smoothly to the great satisfaction of the client.

Turnover had grown, and business was going very well.

I must be honest in saying that I was never as emotionally attached to the Agrate work group as I was to the group of guys in Catania.

In Catania, I had the sensation and the proof that the guys wanted to make a living at all costs.

The guys in Agrate, as good as they were at work, gave more the idea that if something went wrong, the Milan area would support them, and therefore they were less attentive.

In my opinion, they put in less effort than those in Catania.

Unfortunately, as always happens in life, after the ascent, there is always a descent.

The decline also came for our Italian team.

Personally, at the end of 2000, I retired, but I stayed on to manage the business as CEO under a consultancy contract.

I must say that the decision to "leave the field a bit," more than out of necessity, was dictated by pride.

The company changed hands at the end of 2000; Olin split the business, putting all the specialty chemicals (about 1 billion in worldwide business) into the newly formed Arch Chemicals, while leaving the activities called "commodities" in Olin, including Winchester (yes, the one with the rifles), special metals, and more, with a turnover also close to 1 billion US$.

At the same time, I was responsible for Winchester Licensing Europe; in other words, do you remember the highly advertised watch? Well, that was made under license

of the brand, for which I managed the activity as head of licensing in Europe.

Pierre, whether spontaneously or not, decided to retire, and I lost a formidable mentor.

Philippe, General Manager Europe, was called to the USA and became President of Arch Chemical worldwide.

Philippe and I knew each other very well and had great mutual esteem. We worked very hard for the company's fortune.

I must say that in view of my 60 years, it is difficult to float in organizations that need to grow new managers for their future. I felt a bit diminished inside and not in a position to give what I knew I could still give. Laura, the legendary Laura, told me, they haven't understood that they should give you a mission that's doomed from the start. Then they would realize.

Philippe was always very close to me, but I must say that he also showed consideration by avoiding difficult trips or exertions for my somewhat fragile health. Diabetes is a bad disease, even when it is well controlled. Unfortunately, in my job, this was impossible.

Controlling diabetes while traveling with frequent business dinners and all that traveling entails is certainly not very easy.

Philippe asked me to support him at ST in Singapore. As president, he also had responsibility for that area. Thus, on a couple of occasions, he also asked me to accompany him to China, to Beijing and Shanghai.

It was a very diplomatic job done at the top levels of the companies we were in contact with. China is a vast and very beautiful country that can offer many business opportunities. Just think of the mega microelectronics productions that have been built in that country.

Being present there is essential for the company's future.

The history of our activity in Italy (which I care about more than any other) was heading towards an unstoppable decline. At the end of 2004,

Arch Chemical sold its worldwide microelectronics business to the Japanese company Fujifilm Corporation.

Fuji has always been at the forefront, not only in the photography sector but also in microelectronics products. Fuji exclusively marketed the same products as Arch Chemicals in some areas of the Far East. Fuji Hunt and Arch Chemicals were linked by a JV that allowed them to exclusively market products in some areas and to exchange technology between the R&D departments of the two companies. Yes, because Fuji Hunt always had its own R&D, which received support from the enormous R&D of Fuji Co.

In the last 10 years, the only innovative products actually came from that Japanese laboratory and not from the States.

Fuji had a global turnover of 70 billion dollars, making it a huge company.

Fuji could also better guarantee the microelectronics client because it had the possibility and desired to invest in research.

Investments in this sector are very expensive compared to the potential available market worldwide.

Furthermore, three very negative factors for our products began:

the first was that the semiconductor market was no longer growing as in the past, moving towards zero growth.

This triggered a downward price war.

Manufacturers, in turn, to sufficiently reduce costs to sustain very low prices, were forced to act on the products used per unit of finished product, which reached 40%.

This was also possible with the market introduction of equipment that allowed very accurate control of dispensed quantities.

Clients all asked to lower prices with discounts of 10% and more.

Things had become very difficult, and all colleagues blessed the moment Fuji decided to buy the business from Arch.

Fuji, for its part, was suffering from a difficult period because electronic photography had become a reality. And although Fuji was among the first to ride the wave of quality electronic cameras, it had to present a very serious restructuring plan for photography, which certainly also had to involve microelectronics.

I visited the Fujifilm plants in Shizouka, Japan, and I could see firsthand the commitment and capital employed, the working method, and the impeccable organization that are the basis of so many innovative products put on the market.

However, when the market is slow, there are problems for everyone!

At the beginning of 2005, just after the purchase of the business, it was announced that CMS was not part of the package and would therefore remain with Arch.

In Italy, only 6 people plus myself, who had been appointed administrator, president, and CEO of the new company, transferred to Fuji.

The same day, I resigned from the board of Arch Italiana.

Philippe, who had been at the base of the negotiation between the two corporations, was appointed president for the companies in the United States and Europe. The Japanese side created a separate organization (although matrixed with the American one) with its own president and organization.

Arch Chemical, which until that moment still managed the CMS activities in Italy, asked Fuji, through a company contract, to be able to use our experience to exit the CMS activity.

That decision by Arch was because, with the sale of the main business, it no longer made sense to remain only in services.

Contacts to sell the specific activity to a large French group were undertaken; everyone worked hard, but after that, the negotiation failed.

Unfortunately, that was what I feared most because, on the one hand, even under those conditions, we had to guarantee the service to the client, otherwise, there would be enormous damages. On the other hand, if we had closed down, we would have been forced to lay off all the people, sell the assets as best as possible, and leave the company dormant until the lawyers had settled everything that needed to be done in that case.

In the end, we laid off a large part of the staff, incentivizing them with economic aid to the best of Arch's ability.

Laura and I were designated by Arch to handle this aspect and to be the interface for all union activities, which were absolutely necessary in these cases and, moreover, well-regulated by law.

For this, we were helped by a very famous law firm in Milan, which dedicated a lawyer almost full-time to us.

The goal was to do our best by trying to help the exit of those guys who had given their blood to create this activity, while on the other hand, fully respecting the managerial mandate received from Arch.

I believe we fulfilled our task well, as in the end, everyone declared themselves satisfied.

Above all, Laura and I felt clear in our conscience.

Furthermore, the large French group took over the service from Arch, and thus they hired a significant number of the people who had lost their jobs. Laura and I were very sad; this time, we had accompanied one of our creations to the graveyard.

An effort of 11 years. But what troubled us even more was that we hadn't been able to do anything to help all those guys who had placed so much personal trust in us.

We had said goodbye to them one by one, handing them the layoff letter and the last paycheck.

Almost all of them, like me, were very moved by the lost job and by the certainty that it had been an excellent period.

They had gone from people seeking a first job, all recent high school graduates and university graduates, to people with great specialization. They understood this.

Our company, unlike many others, chose to refuse to ask the market for only graduates and diploma holders with experience.

Apart from three or four cases for which it was impossible to do otherwise, Olin Hunt and Arch invested in young people. But if this were not done, who would hire recent high school or university graduates?

Our company invested in these guys by often sending them for training at our plants in Rhode Island and Phoenix, Arizona.

In addition to technical knowledge, we also gave them knowledge of how to operate with multinational companies.

I was behind this choice because I remembered well that when I was young, someone had invested in me!

Anyone in my profession who has experienced laying off fathers knows that it is truly traumatic. It is nice to hire, but terrible to layoff.

The faces of the people you tell they have lost their job are unforgettable.

The year 2006 thus marked a turning point in my working life, and for the first time, from being a person at the height of my career, I felt useless.

My potential was still intact, but the job no longer required my effort.

Hence, a significant onset of frustration.

I talked about it with Philippe, but he too was starting to have his own problems and could do nothing to reverse the situation that was developing.

We had all always worked with American organizations and were therefore little prepared for a sudden change caused by working for a Japanese company.

The mentality, the way of understanding and doing things are totally different.

Language barriers become important. The English spoken by an American or a European is absolutely different from the English spoken by the Japanese.

Apart from high-level managers, with other colleagues, we hardly understood each other at all. Every sentence said or heard had to be repeated or made to be repeated at least three times to get an idea if they had understood well what was said or heard.

To try to understand their culture, companies, in these situations, organize real courses with Japanese teachers.

This is not a criticism; it is just an observation.

The relationship between Philippe and the top management of Fuji had become problematic; I witnessed this during a meeting in Japan at Fuji headquarters when I observed a significant disagreement.

In March 2007, Philippe left his job. He was prepared for this and was already working on restructuring a beautiful villa on the French Riviera where he planned to spend the summers resting.

I was under psychological pressure from my management, who made me understand that things would end.

A significant push towards the end of my working experience certainly came from the subordinate colleagues who, in my departure, rightly saw an opportunity for career growth for themselves.

As they say, when one pope dies, another must be made!

Laura definitively retired at the same time Philippe stopped.

She was greeted with great respect, and we organized two dinners with colleagues, one in Belgium and one in Milan.

Laura was a cornerstone for our activity.

Philippe is the person I have met who has traveled the most, absolutely.

Now the family will have to help him slow down gradually. It's not easy after a lifetime at those rhythms!

He was replaced as president by Jim LC, also a colleague I knew well and who was talented.

I too have traveled a lot for work.

I have been to all of North America, Europe, Israel, the socialist countries, India, Thailand, the Philippines, South Korea, Hong Kong, Taipei, Malaysia, Japan, and China.

My experience in Africa is limited to South Africa and Ethiopia.

I have never traveled to Australia or South America anf New Zeland.

Traveling for work meant above all learning to navigate all airports, hotels where you stay, and restaurants.

Travel, meetings, one or two nights in a hotel, and then back. Sightseeing? Rarely.

One of my expectations as a retiree is to return to places I have already been with my wife to revisit these places as a tourist. I think I will discover so many new things!

Traveling, on the other hand, has given me the opportunity to meet many famous people. This is especially true in airports.

The most pleasant encounter was with the Dalai Lama at Rome Fiumicino Airport about 9 years ago.

I was arriving from Singapore to Milan with Emirates, which made an intermediate stop in Rome after Dubai.

I was suffering from terrible back pain that prevented me from standing. The stopover was expected to last about two hours.

I was sitting on the chairs in front of the gate with other people, and to my right, there was an empty seat but with newspapers placed on it. It was summer and hot, and I was tired from the journey, which had already lasted 12 hours up to that point.

Suddenly, a gentleman and a lady dressed in gray (typical of VIP escorts at the airport) asked me if the seat next to me was free. I nodded and instinctively gathered and put aside the newspapers that were lying on it, left by other travelers.

At that point, I looked up and saw a gentleman who sat down next to me, dressed in the typical orange robe. It was the Dalai Lama! I couldn't believe my eyes! Think about it, it was like finding myself sitting next to our Pope!

I recognized him immediately, stood up, and greeted him with a bow. The other passengers, seeing me in that posture, also recognized him. I tried to speak with him in the 3 languages I know well, but he smiled at me with dignity and gave me a nod with his head but did not speak a word. Then I promptly offered him my business card (the most senseless thing I have ever done... but it was the emotion) and he gently put it in his worn black leather V-opening document bag and, in turn, pulled out his, which was a handwritten business card that bore his name Tenzin Gyatso (that is his name) with the address in Mcleod Ganj, India, of the monastery where he lives.

I noticed that above his left eyebrow, just above his glasses, he had a small mole. When I got home, I immediately went online, downloaded a photo of him, and had confirmation, from the small mole I had noticed, that that day I touched the hand and had the honor of meeting in person a great man whom I have followed ever since.

Returning to Philippe, the evening the announcement was made that he was ending his presidency of the company, while driving towards Grenoble near Bardonecchia, with Fiorella and my beloved little grandchild, I felt a very strong pain in my chest.

I didn't know if it was a cold draft that had caused a digestion blockage or a heart attack.

I always traveled with a small supply of medicines, including Trinitrina, a potent vasodilator, to be used in such cases. I immediately took a pill under my tongue.

But I opted for the cold draft theory.

In reality, I wasn't well; I felt that something serious was happening to me!

The next morning, I left Fiorella and Jaiden at the hotel while I went to the very important business meeting.

I felt very weak, but in the end, I continued to work as if nothing had happened.

I continued to work for about 15 days, going back and forth from clients and to Belgium. However, I realized that something was wrong because I got tired very easily and was short of breath.

Finally, I decided to get a checkup at the Clinica Santa Rita in Milan. I have used this institution for 30 years and have always been very satisfied.

They admitted me, and as soon as they did the echocardiogram, they informed me that I was having a heart attack.

For double verification, they did a specific enzyme analysis, and this also confirmed everything!

The head of cardiology, Professor Angelo Anzuini, an excellent person to whom I truly owe my life, told me that the following morning he would perform an angiogram with contrast to evaluate the extent of the cardiac damage.

That night was truly long. I felt like someone awaiting execution, to be carried out the next morning.

I suddenly realized that my time for reckoning had arrived.

The film starts from today and goes back to the days when, as a young man, I was desperately searching for a job to be able to fulfill myself in life, sending all those job applications that systematically received a "no thank you, our staff is full!"

In my case, I was lucky, but I must say that I did everything I could to help luck help me!

To return to myself. That morning I was treated, and they put in 4 stents, "balloons with treated metal cages to widen the right coronary artery."

The intervention had been very difficult due to the extent of the coronary occlusion and lasted 5 hours instead of the usual one hour, and it was done on a conscious patient. I was very calm because I immediately understood that I was in good hands and my professor was a person who knows his job well. During the intervention, he continued to talk to me. This gave me confidence, and it helped him understand if I was tolerating the intervention well.

I was a heavy smoker, but that time I threw away the cigarettes, and after (now) 5 and half years, I can say that I have not touched one since.

This is to tell those who don't want to quit that it is possible, and it would be better to decide to quit when you are not forced by a matter of life or death. What do you say? In life, there is always something to learn.

In hindsight, even the most difficult decisions to make become relatively easy!

After the stent procedure, I recovered very well and had a completely normal working and private life for another three years.

Meanwhile, Prof. Anzuini performed some preventive maintenance interventions, such as ablation of the central coronary artery, widening its diameter and reinforcing it with two new stents.

Total now I have six stents.

After the six-month checkup via angiography, the doctor verified that the last two stents were not perfectly contiguous and left a space in between where new deposits could proliferate on the wall.

Thus, a new stent was implanted, total number 7.

I didn't lose heart, and after some time, I returned to work, but the road was uphill.

Life, thanks to God and my highly experienced cardiologist and primary care doctor, Dr. Sartirana, continued, and I had not stopped being happy and continuing to love life to the best of my ability.

The ending.

In recent times, the financial crisis, which would last for a long time yet, began to be felt.

Often in my reflections, I tried to compare my period before and after all these years, and this, especially having three children and three grandchildren, made it normal to wonder what future these young lives would have.

I firmly believe that the problems my generation had to face are not very different from those that today's young people must and will face.

Then as now, the major problem was having a job that provided a certain income upon which the family could build and thus be in a position to plan their future.

Today in Italy, the permanent job has almost disappeared, and if you lose your job, even a permanent one, it is difficult to be re-employed quickly, especially if you are over 50 years old.

In short, it is so difficult to cope with the present and plan the future.

Often young people stay at home with their parents until they are thirty and beyond, and often, alas, they are already retirees because they use their parents' pension money to live!

But what choices have our political leaders made and are they making?

Unfortunately, it is a global problem, and no one seems to have the definitive solution to the problem in the short term.

However, a bit of foresight and some courageous choices would have certainly helped to do better.

Unfortunately, I believe that without a new, enthusiastic, and young political class, none of the above will be resolved.

Returning to my work, I had the first signs that my company had put me on the departure list in November 2007. By then, I had recovered from my illness, but I was no longer able to exert myself as before. I had to take care of myself. Note that for the heart attack, I was absent from work for a total of, perhaps, 10 days. Today, however, with a PC and a phone nearby, one can work efficiently from anywhere, and therefore also from home as a convalescent.

However, I knew that the contract as administrator and chairman of the board of directors, which was renewed on a two-year basis, was coming to an end. On the other hand, I had already been retired for 7 years. The signs that the job was about to end continued until June 2008.

All kinds of pessimism were coming from the global financial world. Large insurance companies and some American banks failed.

As already said, it was the beginning of the global economic crisis, which is still ongoing today, more serious than the great American crisis at the beginning of the last century.

Everyone was preparing plans to cut costs, and everyone did so.

I was the simplest case because I was hired on contract.

On October 30th, at the request of the Japanese shareholder, I resigned as administrator of the company and stayed home.

In short, I was fired.

It would have been more fulfilling to leave the company with great fanfare, but I realize that having retired at the beginning of 2001 and continued until the end of 2008 as a consultant with identical managerial functions, I could consider myself satisfied.

That's life... and it must be taken as it comes with the saying... if you have a problem and there is a solution, why get angry? And if there is no solution, why get angry?

True in words but difficult to swallow.

However, the fact remains that I have given a good contribution to the companies I worked for, and here, my conscience is on my side!

But that's not all.

In the summer of 2010, after returning from a visit to Fiorella's mother in Ethiopia, I felt ill again, a lump in my throat. It immediately appeared as a kind of angina, but I wasn't sure, so in the middle of the night, I decided to call 118 (emergency services), explaining my previous heart issues, the current symptoms, and begging them to intervene as soon as possible.

I hung up the phone, and for about a couple of minutes, I dozed off on the sofa. Suddenly, I woke up with a jolt, stood up, and began counting on my fingertips aloud up to three. I remember this well.

My wife told me that after pronouncing "three," I collapsed to the ground, gasping, with cardiopulmonary arrest. Fortunately, at that precise moment, as my wife later told me, the 118 personnel rang the gate bell, and shortly after, they diagnosed me with cardiopulmonary arrest.

I was virtually dead. My heart was no longer beating, and my lungs were rattling without exchanging any oxygen with the bloodstream.

Fortunately, the operators had a defibrillator and what was needed to restart my heart and begin the slow reoxygenation of the blood.

I was intubated and transported to Vimercate Hospital in code red, where I remained in a pharmaceutical coma in the intensive care unit for 10 days, followed by another 10 days in a room. Fiorella told me that at the intensive care unit, they did the impossible to keep me alive with wonderful professionalism, dedication, and kindness that we often don't imagine can exist in our hospitals. Thanks to all of them, I am still here to finish this story, two years after the event.

After a month, I was discharged, and in the meantime, they put two more stents in the left branch of the coronary arteries, reaching a total of 9 in three years.

Let's hope that these blessed stents remain open for some time yet!

The thing to note is that I am not at all scared. The transition from alive to virtually dead happened without pain or any sensation. If dying happens this way, dying is less traumatic than we imagine;

Unlike many others, I don't remember anything about lights at the end of the tunnel, much less someone who took my hand and led me back to life.

In short, absolute nothingness until I woke up from the coma.

I think that was not my time, and that's it. I believe a little in destiny that orders our life path.

When I reopened my eyes, I saw Fiorella bent over me, and I asked what had happened to me. She said, "Welcome back to me!"

Fiorella says it is a warning and means that I am still expected to do something important in life!

Now, however, I am well, and I have learned better how to live and seize the small joys that life offers me every day.

I firmly believe that life consists of a few very firm rules, the main one being respect for others, but certainly not the last one being to do everything lawfully possible to procure the maximum happiness for ourselves.

To avoid the rigors of the winter cold, Fiorella and I decided to buy a house in Florida where we spend a part of the winter period where the climate is always mild and therefore pleasant and livable, especially for people with heart conditions like me.

I must say that I like being there very much, especially because I have met in our neighbors, more or less all my peers, so much friendship and company. In most cases, they are retired corporate executives, and like me, they have many stories and time to exchange with each other.

Life flows well there, and I have my own; I have learned to slow it down a lot!

The frantic business trips are now a distant memory.

You retire, and after some time, even for people always as active as me, you learn to be a retiree.

You learn to meditate, and you become professors of "What if," meaning what would have happened if instead of doing this, I had done something else?

This is why old age is the period of life's reckoning.

The film of what has been lived is seen and reviewed many times. The conclusions that seem valid to us one day do not always hold true for the following days.

The important thing is to always be well with oneself. If we like ourselves a little, then we are well with ourselves.

I believe that at the end of all this struggling in life, we know that the time for reckoning will come, and at that moment, still alive, we want to like ourselves.

Perhaps this is what we should all wish for ourselves and possibly make others understand, especially the young.

But I truly believe I am not the first to have these reflections.

The difference is that when I had them as a young person, they were made by others; now, instead, they come from within me and from my life experience.

I would not want to put an end to this story of my life yet, as I would like to continue living it a bit, continuing to thank it for having given me so much through all the situations and experiences it has given me with full hands.

In fact, I feel very satisfied, and I am a happy person.

Today is Christmas Day, here in Florida. It is 24 degrees Celsius outside, and we were waiting for Travis to arrive from Washington DC with his wife Katiria and our two little grandchildren.

Jaiden, my inspiring grandchild, arrived from Maryland three days ago and is also enjoying the sweet, almost summer-like warmth of Florida and the pool that seems tailor-made for him.

As soon as the family was reunited, we began our Christmas lunch that Fiorella had prepared for us with so much dedication, skill, and love.

We prayed together to the good God for having given us the joy of spending this day together.

The children opened the gifts found under the tree, and as soon as lunch was over, they started playing with the presents.

I, like a good "old man," sat on my armchair waiting for my espresso coffee, and with my eyes half-closed,

I began to review the frames of my film that I am telling you about, and without realizing it, I was in tears.

I don't know what is happening to me; perhaps as you get older, tears come more easily, or perhaps as you get older, you become more sensitive.I don't know!

Certainly, I think of the fortune of having lived through this beautiful period, for us of peace, of great discoveries that have truly revolutionized history and the way of life of man.

One evening, I told Jaiden about something that had happened to me as a boy. I told a cheerful story, but I didn't say that I was at the center of the story.

He listened more silently than usual, but, unlike other times, he didn't fall asleep.

He looked at me and said, "All this happened to you, right, Nonni?" (Nonni is grandpa, Americanized)

I replied yes and asked, "Did you understand the meaning?" He looked at me with his splendid eyes and said, "Yes, Nonni," and continued, "You know, I still want these stories of yours because they help me understand many things."

I hope with this writing to fulfill his desire to acquire experience.

This is a short story of a life that is summarized in less than 200 pages. Is an entire life possible in only 200 pages?

Fortunately, mine are 200, but let's remember that they could be even less, much less.

What I have learned and want to possibly transmit is that even in the worst situations; one must never lose heart and be well aware that, as I have already written above, God never disturbs the happiness of men without guaranteeing them a greater and more lasting one.

This will make you find the strength to always win!

Willpower and perseverance is the key to everything.

But not secondary, although I mention it last, is respect for others, just as our religion has always taught us.

With this cocktail, my grandchild and young people like him will successfully change the way they live and will be very happy about it.

Then I asked myself the concluding question: Giuliano, would you do it all over again? I answer the question without hesitation with a full yes; I would do everything, absolutely yes, everything, truly everything.

This writing has never been published, and I only reviewed it in April 2025. And the Good God and my great fortune, after everything that has happened to me, I am still among you. Now I am over 81 years old. I waited a long time before deciding to put the final word on the book.

Now, after finishing it, I will put it away printed, and in the future, if the good God leaves me a little longer with you, and when my memory begins to falter, then I will pick it up and, by rereading it, it will help me to always remember that however hard life may be, it is always a great gift from God and must be lived and savored to the last drop, just like good wine!

This is how my life was, simply a life!

After all, Proust is right; writing about your life is reliving it.

I dedicate this writing to Fiorella, to my children Amanda, Travis, and Brian, to my deceased brother Piero, to my sister-in-law Luciana, and to my nephews Mauro and Alessandro, but particularly to my grandchildren Jaiden, Nathan, Adriana, Melanie, Nolan and to all those who have supported me and loved me and whom I have loved in my life, to whom, even if not mentioned here, I am very grateful.

Have a good life to all of you who have had the patience to read me to the end.

Thank you, I love you.